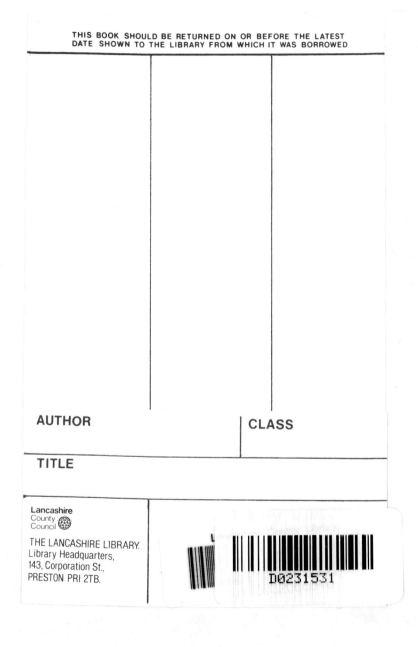

THIS BOOK SHOULD BE RETURNED ON OR BEFORE THE LATEST
DATE SHOWN TO THE LIBRARY FROM WHICH IT WAS BORROWED

AUTHOR

CLASS

TITLE

The Year After the Fair

A Play

Donald Madgwick

Samuel French – London
New York – Sydney – Toronto – Hollywood

THE YEAR AFTER THE FAIR

First presented by St. Mark's and Keston Players on 5th November, 1987, with the following cast of characters:

Henry Harnham	Brian Etheridge
Edith Harnham	Hazel Parry
Charles Raye	Denis Hitchcock
Anna Raye	Viv O'Keefe
Arnold Slocombe	Jonathan Farley
Betty	Melanie Arnold
Thomas Hardy	Hylton Clark
Charlotte Raye	Jean Middleton

The play directed by Joan Dutton

The action of the play takes place in the drawing-room of the Harnhams' house in Salisbury.

ACT I	SCENE 1	An afternoon in March
	SCENE 2	Morning, several weeks later
	SCENE 3	Early evening, several days later
	SCENE 4	The following afternoon
ACT II	SCENE 1	An afternoon in October
	SCENE 2	Early evening, several days later
	SCENE 3	Later the same evening

Time—the late 19th century

CHARACTERS

Henry Harnham, a wine merchant
Edith Harnham, his wife
Charles Raye, a barrister
Anna Raye, his wife
Arnold Slocombe, a wine merchant
Betty, the Harnhams' maid
Thomas Hardy, a novelist
Charlotte Raye, Charles' sister

To Joan Dutton, who nagged . . .

ACT I

SCENE 1

The drawing-room of the house of Henry and Edith Harnham in Salisbury

The year is 1893, and the furnishings and atmosphere reflect the period, high summer of the British Empire, and also Henry's self-satisfied pride in his standing and possessions. The walls are adorned with portraits and conventional landscapes. Objects, mainly of an ornamental nature, decorate a sideboard R *and a small table* L. US *is a heavily-curtained window looking out at the Cathedral and the city square. A door* L *leads to the hall and thence to the street. A bell-rope is conveniently situated. Furnishings include a small, low-backed settee, chairs, another small table and a writing-desk* UR. *A piano is optional*

When the CURTAIN *rises, it is early afternoon of a day in March. Henry and Edith are discovered. Henry is a self-important, middle-aged man of business, his wife an attractive lady of around thirty with a natural grace and dignity. The contrast between their moods is at once apparent. He is seated on the settee, quite relaxed, reading a paper while she paces the room, barely able to contain her impatience. At length she comes to rest by the window, where she stands gazing out into the square.*

Henry lays down his paper and addresses her in a testy tone of voice

Henry Do come away from that window, Edith. Posting yourself as look-out will not bring them here any quicker.

Edith (*more to herself than to him*) I was thinking ...

Henry I believe you do too much thinking. I don't approve of this marriage at all. It was your thinking that got them into it.

Edith (*as before*) How quiet the square looks now. How peaceful.

Henry Thank goodness for that. I suppose you were remembering that dreadful fair they had there last autumn. That was where it all started, wasn't it?

Edith (*coming out of her reverie*) I beg your pardon.

Henry The fair. Was it not at the fair that Anna met that young fellow Raye?

Edith Yes. Yes, it was.

Henry Never did hold with them myself. Nasty, noisy machinery. Vulgar people. All manner of shady things going on.

Edith (*mildly*) They met innocently enough.

Henry And just look what it led to. If that was an innocent meeting, I wonder what you would call a guilty one.

Edith What's past is done. The girl was very inexperienced.

Henry (*irritably*) I really do marvel at you, Edith. When I married you, I thought you had decent standards like the rest of us. These modern ideas of yours!

Edith This is eighteen ninety-three, Henry, not the Middle Ages. Is it modern to feel for a girl whose enthusiasm outruns her discretion?

Henry Well, he'll have married her by now. Unless he changed his mind at the last minute.

Edith What time is it?

Henry (*looking at his pocket-watch*) Almost two-thirty.

Edith The train should be in by now.

Henry I expect so.

Edith I wonder you didn't go to the station to meet them.

Henry The fly is perfectly efficient.

Edith I was thinking of courtesy, not efficiency.

Henry (*offended*) Courtesy!

Edith I would have gone myself, but you told me it would not be seemly.

Henry What are you thinking of? Anna was your *maid*. I'll tell you what is seemly: that Anna should come to *you*.

Edith Anna *was* my maid. She's now Mrs Charles Bradford Raye, wife of a rising London barrister.

He rises and struts about, the picture of self-important indignation

Henry Bah! The whole thing's preposterous. The most absurd match that ever was made. A simple serving girl marrying a professional man. And all through your agency.

Edith (*flushing*) How can you say that?

Henry I daresay you helped her with her letters. I wasn't aware the girl could even write. I do know she doesn't have the wit to compose the kind of letters that would win the heart of a barrister.

Edith Have you forgotten the girl is pregnant?

Henry How can you be so simple, Edith? Do you fancy such a man would risk his whole career just because a silly little girl tricks him into making her pregnant? She could have gone to live with that old aunt of hers. I'm sure Raye would have made provision for the child.

Edith He did the honourable thing.

Henry Well, I must confess I'm baffled. (*He sits down with exaggerated dignity*) I don't want to sound self-important, but I suppose I've built up the most prosperous wine business in this part of the country.

Edith What about Arnold Slocombe?

Henry You leave Arnold Slocombe to me, my dear. Running the house is your concern. I know how the world works. And I know promising young barristers don't marry serving girls just because their indiscretions lead to, er, certain consequences.

Edith You have much to learn, Henry, for all your worldliness.

Henry Sit down, Edith.

She sits at the writing-desk

Now. I suggest you tell me about these letters.

Edith What's there to tell? Mr Raye visited the fair and met Anna. They had a brief liaison. He went back to London and wrote to her.

Henry And that started the whole damnable train of events. *Did* you help her to compose those letters, Edith?

Edith (*looking away*) Well, perhaps I, er, helped her a little.

Henry May one ask in what way?

Edith (*coldly*) I may be your wife, Henry, but I'm not your servant. I have helped Anna in many ways. I would remind you that I took her under my protection without consulting you.

Henry Which made her your responsibily. Is this how you discharge it? By encouraging her in a course that can only lead to disaster?

Edith On the contrary, I did my best to *discourage* her.

Henry Well, we shall see.

There is the sound of a fly stopping, off. Edith goes to the window

Edith They are here. There is the fly. They are alighting. Henry, can we not lay aside our incessant disagreements and greet them joyfully?

Henry (*stiffly*) You know I have prepared a reception for them in the dining-room.

Edith (*more softly*) Yes, Henry. It was very good of you. But please don't spoil it by ...

Henry By what?

Edith Nothing. I'm sure you know the forms.

Henry (*with a touch of sarcasm*) How kind of you to say so.

Charles and Anna enter, dressed for travelling. He is a pleasant young man in his late twenties, she a pretty creature many years his junior, just now greatly excited and eager to please

Charles (*shaking hands in turn*) Mr Harnham. Mrs Harnham.

Henry We are glad to welcome you, Mr Raye.

Charles We are much obliged. Aren't we, Anna?

Anna (*speaking quickly, which emphasizes her soft regional accent*) Oh, Mr Harnham, sir—and you, dear mistress—I feel so excited. For we were married this morning, you know, at the Register Office in London, and now I'm Mrs Charles Raye, and isn't it a lovely day for it and all?

Charles (*good-naturedly*) Do pause for breath now and again, my dear.

Edith You are looking quite radiant, Anna. And you must not call me your mistress any more.

Anna Dear Charles, she was so kind to me, you know, when——

Charles (*cutting in*) Yes, I know. But you will have to get used to your new status in life.

Edith You were always so impulsive, Anna.

Henry I'll leave you three to talk while I go and see to the reception.

Henry exits

Edith So now you are well and truly married.

Charles Show her the ring, Anna.

Anna removes her glove

Anna (*holding up her left hand*) There, is it not the prettiest of rings? I can't
believe it's on my finger. I thought I should wake up and find it all a
dream.

Charles Mrs Harnham, you must excuse my darling wife. She does prattle
on so. Anna, my dear, you've hardly stopped talking since we left
London.

Anna (*contritely*) I must learn to hold my tongue.

Edith Did you have a good journey?

Charles The railway service was excellent, thank you.

Anna I counted the cows.

Edith (*smiling*) A most demanding occupation, I'm sure. Mr Raye, I hope
you and Anna will stay the night before proceeding on your honeymoon.

Charles It will be a pleasure. We are going to Bournemouth, you know.

Edith A charming resort. And suitably quiet at this time of year. What do
you think, Anna?

Anna I'm sure I don't know. I never was there in my life. Charles chose it.

Edith I hope you will always choose things together from now on.

Charles (*lightly*) Oh, I'm sure Anna has firm opinions on all manner of
things. Haven't you, my dear?

Anna I only want to do what's best for you.

Charles Mrs Harnham, my wife is rather flurried at present. She needs a
little rest. It will not be long, I'm certain, before her tongue finds that
charming philosophy which her lovely letters revealed.

Edith (*turning away; embarrassed*) Of course. And now I must go to the
reception. I'll leave you two alone for a few minutes before you join us.

Edith exits hurriedly

Anna Shouldn't we go as well?

Charles All in good time. You are back in your old surroundings now. You
are not too tired for the reception, I hope.

Anna Oh, no, I'm not a bit tired. I'll be the life and soul.

Charles Good. It was very kind of Mr Harnham to provide it. But first, I
have a trifling task for you.

Anna Anything you say, dear Charles.

Charles As you know, my sister Charlotte was unable to attend the
wedding. She is indisposed at present.

Anna I know. I was so looking forward to meeting her.

Charles Plenty of time for that in the future. I know you and she are going
to be the best of friends. You will find her advice invaluable when it comes
to domestic arrangements. She is such a practical person.

Anna (*somewhat put out*) I know what's what.

Charles Of course you do. Yet you would do well to acknowledge her
experience in these matters. A married professional man needs to do a
certain amount of entertaining.

Anna What was the task you had for me?

Charles (*pointing to the writing-desk*) Sit down there, Anna dear.

She sits at the desk, looking apprehensive

That's right. Do you have pen and paper?

Anna (*uneasily*) Pen and paper?

Charles Yes. I want you to write a short note to my sister.

Anna Oh, Charles, must I?

Charles Of course you must. It's common courtesy.

Anna (*pouting*) But I'm so tired.

Charles You said just now you were not in the least tired. Come along, Anna, you must thank her for the present she sent you. Tell her you hope to know her well, for she is now sister to both of us.

Anna (*pen in hand, miserably*) Oh, Charles . . .

Charles And couch your letter in the pretty, poetical way that comes so naturally to you in correspondence. (*He is not looking directly at her, and does not observe her agitation*) It was your letters that cemented the bond between us. We met here in Salisbury last October, at the fair. I first caught a glimpse of you on the hobby-horse. Do you remember?

Anna How could I ever forget?

Charles (*reliving the moment*) Round and round you went, bobbing up and down. You looked so happy. As if the world had no greater pleasure to offer.

Anna I'd never been to a fair before.

Charles (*at the window*) It was there, in that very square, close by the cathedral. I remember marvelling at the contrast. The cloistered calm of many centuries, and the lurid racket of this one. We met, and came together under those garish lights.

Anna (*reliving the moment also*) Oh, yes. Dear Charles.

Charles Yet for me, at the time—I must be frank—it was no more than the dalliance of the moment.

Anna It's what's happened since. That's all that matters.

Charles Yes, you are right. I busy in London, you with your work down here. I fell in love with you through your letters.

Anna (*hanging her head*) Oh, yes, my letters . . .

Charles comes behind her and takes her hand

Charles Never had I read such letters in my life.

Anna averts her gaze, a gesture he misreads as a modest disclaimer

No, Anna, this is no idle flattery. I had expected extravagance and vulgarity. And I found a magical simplicity and the tenderest of sentiments. Nothing insincere, nothing overstated. You have a rare gift, Anna. I hope you know it.

Anna (*turning to him with tears in her eyes*) But, Charles, surely you would still have loved me without the letters?

Charles What makes you say that?

Anna For myself, I mean.

Charles Exactly. For that self you showed in the letters.

Anna But without them?

Charles Of course you were bright and attractive. I noticed *that* at the fair. But the question is hypothetical.

Anna Hypo ... ?

Charles The letters *exist*. I have them in my travelling bag, every one. How could I not fall in love with the writer of such gems?

Anna Charles, can't we go to the reception?

Charles Of course. When you have written to my sister.

Anna Can't it wait?

Charles If I didn't know you better, Anna, I might suspect you were hiding something. Come along, we haven't got all day. You know well enough what to say.

She screws her face up in an attitude of frowning concentration. He draws away and paces up and down as she begins to make imprints on the paper. Presently, he comes to the desk to see how far she has progressed

Why, Anna, what's this?

Anna (*in tears*) Oh, Charles, I—I can't do it any better!

Charles (*angrily*) What nonsense is this? Pull yourself together, girl!

Anna (*hysterically; banging her fist on the desk*) I can't, I can't, I *can't*!

Charles Can't?

Anna You'll have to know the truth. I didn't write those letters!

Charles (*slowly, in a stunned voice*) You didn't write them?

Anna (*rising and stamping her foot in anger and despair*) No, I tell you, no! I got *her* to write them!

Charles Her? Mrs Harnham?

Anna (*desperately trying to salvage something*) But I told her what to put. Well, sometimes. And I'm sure she always wrote what I said, except that some of the *words* may have been hers, and—and——

Charles (*icily*) Anna, are you telling me you are illiterate?

Anna I'm learning, dear Charles. So fast you wouldn't believe it. She's been teaching me. I've been practising every day. (*She lifts her face, her eyes stained with tears*) Dear husband, you will forgive me, won't you? I meant to tell you before, but things just went on, and—and—oh, I *meant* to tell you, honest!

Charles tears in two the letter she has been trying to write and drops it on the desk. He hands her a handkerchief and speaks in a cold, formal manner

Charles Here, dry your tears.

Anna dabs her eyes

That's better. You must be looking your best. Now go and join the others.

Anna (*timidly*) And you?

Charles Please tell Mrs Harnham I should like to see her.

Anna Yes, Charles.

Anna exits

Charles watches her go, then stands at the window, looking out

Charles (*under his breadth*) That damned fair. (*He turns away from the window*) All those honeyed letters. What a *fool* I've been. (*He throws himself into a chair and covers his face with both hands*)

It is in this attitude that Edith finds him when she enters a few moments later

Edith Mr Raye. Why, what's the matter?
Charles I think you can guess, Mrs Harnham.

Edith moves swiftly to the desk, sees the torn letter, picks it up, then lets the pieces fall

Edith Oh, no, not that!
Charles So you were her scribe. (*Bitterly*) Or should I say amanuensis? Or dare I say author?
Edith It was . . . necessary.
Charles (*jumping up; greatly agitated*) Necessary! To ruin me?
Edith (*anguished*) Please, Mr Raye, don't!
Charles Come, Mrs Harnham, I must know the full truth. Did she dictate every word you ever wrote to me?
Edith Not every word.
Charles How much? (*Raising his voice*) How much, Mrs Harnham?
Edith I'm sure they echoed her thoughts.
Charles Never mind her thoughts. Did they record her *words*?
Edith Well, not many.
Charles In fact, very few?
Edith I think you could say that.
Charles Let us not prevaricate, Mrs Harnham. *Would* you say that?
Edith Yes.
Charles So the words were yours. And the thoughts.

Edith shrugs helplessly

Please, Mrs Harnham. Won't you sit down?

Edith sits

Now. Tell me the whole story. I must know it all.
Edith I did it out of kindness to the girl.
Charles (*impatiently*) The story, Mrs Harnham, the story!
Edith It began with the letter you sent to her. After your visit to the fair and—and the following three days. You asked her to write. That at least you must admit.
Charles Of course. Go on.
Edith She brought the letter to me.
Charles And asked you to read it?
Edith Yes. And when she knew you wanted her to write, she asked me if I would do it for her.
Charles Without explaining the deception?
Edith (*nodding*) She said she couldn't bear you to think she was not able to do it herself. "I should sink into the earth with shame if he knew that." Those were her exact words.

Charles And then?

Edith By degrees, I was drawn into the correspondence that followed. At first she suggested a few words here and there. I rephrased them, to give a little polish. Then she began leaving things more and more to me. Trusting in my judgment.

Charles (*bleakly*) A trust only too well earned.

Edith Then she told me she was expecting a baby. My husband found out about it and sent her away. To her aunt's cottage on the plain. From then on, I could not even consult her. I replied to your letters, and mailed her copies of yours as they arrived.

Charles What was the good of that, since she couldn't read?

Edith There was a trustworthy neighbour who read them out to her.

Charles Let me be precise about this. You found yourself corresponding, in another's name, under no prompting from her, with a man not your husband, in terms which were virtually those of a wife?

Edith You express it exactly.

Charles Concerning a pregnancy that was to all intents and purposes your own, though actually of another?

Edith hangs her head, saying nothing

God help you, Mrs Harnham! And God help me!

Edith (*crushed*) I tried to save a simple girl from misery.

Charles (*bitterly*) Oh, that must have been *very* hard for you.

Edith I must admit it gave me pleasure also.

Charles (*suddenly alert, his instincts aroused*) Go on, Mrs Harnham. We might as well have the whole truth.

Edith Do you remember that I came looking for Anna at the fair?

Charles nods

We met that day, Mr Raye. Briefly but ... emphatically.

Charles (*low*) How, emphatically?

Edith (*her voice becoming more ardent as she recalls the scene*) There was a sudden surge in the crowd. We all found ourselves pressed tightly together.

Charles That's right. I took Anna's hand. For comfort and reassurance. The way she clung to me, her trust in my strength, made my heart go out to her.

Edith (*very quietly*) It was not Anna's hand you were holding, Mr Raye. It was mine.

Charles (*a quick intake of breath*) Yours!

Edith You went on holding it till the crowd fell away. (*A pause*) I did not withdraw it. (*A longer pause*) Do you now see why that correspondence gave me pleasure?

Charles Only too clearly. You and I, Mrs Harnham, are friends, lovers— deep and devoted lovers—by correspondence. Lovers by proxy.

Edith May God forgive me ... it's true.

Charles And now ... more.

Edith More?

Charles You saw that ring on her finger. Legally I have married her. In soul and spirit I have married you.

Edith You must not say so!

Charles Do you love your husband?

Edith You have no right to ask that!

Charles I have every right. I daresay he's twenty years your senior. Did you ever love him?

Edith He offered me security.

Charles That was not the question.

Edith I have always respected him.

Charles (*agitated*) Oh, yes, respect is easily bought. And so you indulged yourself. You fell in love on someone else's behalf. That's an indulgence, isn't it? Or what else would you call it? Shielding yourself behind a poor illiterate girl. The bond is between you and me, not me and her!

Edith Stop, Charles, stop!

Charles You called me Charles.

Edith Yes.

Charles Tomorrow we leave this house, my bride and I. I shall go out of your life for ever. Before then, I think I have one claim on you.

Edith What claim?

He takes her in his arms. She does not resist

Charles If what you wrote in those letters was fiction, give me your cheek only. If it was true, your lips.

Edith Oh, Charles! (*She kisses him passionately on the mouth*) Can you forgive me, Charles?

Charles I forgive you, Edith.

Edith But you are ruined ...

Charles Then you owe me one more. One last embrace.

They kiss, with even greater passion. When they withdraw from each other's arms it is slowly and with obvious reluctance

Edith That was a mad thing to do.

Charles Was it? I shall never see you again.

Edith Do you suppose women forget so easily?

Charles Do you suppose men don't remember?

Edith (*to the door*) I must go.

Charles Wait.

She turns

I have one more request. Just now, I asked Anna to write a brief note to my sister Charlotte. She was indisposed, and unable to come to the ceremony. I wanted Anna to thank her for the present she sent—to call her "sister"—to look forward to her future friendship.

Edith And that was how you learned the truth?

Charles Yes. I would like you to write that letter, Edith. For Anna. As you wrote to me.

Edith (*sitting at the desk and taking up a pen*) Charlotte, you say?

Charles Miss Charlotte Raye. Address her "Dear Sister".
Edith Very well.

She writes with great rapidity while Charles talks

Charles This will be your last service to me, Edith. Our final contact. My
business takes me on the Western Circuit two or three times a year, but a
meeting would be most unwise. I shall of course destroy your letters. I
must learn to play the role of husband to your serving-maid. Any
reminders of how I came to be cast would be most painful. Perhaps I shall
give up my profession altogether. Can you picture me as a small
shopkeeper?
Edith (*blotting the letter and handing it to him*) There, will that do?
Charles I was talking to myself, I see. Just as well, perhaps. (*Reading*) "Dear
Sister—Charles and I were so sorry you could not . . ." (*His voice lowers to
a murmur until he comes to the end*) "Very truly yours, for and on behalf
of Anna Raye—Edith Harnham." What's this? For and on behalf of?
Edith No more deceptions, Charles.
Charles Of course. You are right. No more deceptions.

Anna enters

Anna (*entering*) Charles, they're all waiting for you.
Charles Yes, Anna, I'm coming.
Anna What's that paper you're holding?
Charles A letter to my sister. Penned by a lady of proven competence.
Anna (*warmly*) Oh, dear mistress, I knew I could depend on you. (*To
Charles*) She has such a way with her, such a touch.
Charles (*with an irony she could not possibly appreciate*) Has she, now?
After you, Mrs Harnham. Come, Anna.

They all leave for the reception as——

—the CURTAIN *falls*

SCENE 2

The same. A bright morning in early May, several weeks later

*Henry enters, followed by Arnold Slocombe, a man of about forty with an
easy, attractive manner*

Henry Come in, Slocombe, come in.

Henry motions Arnold to the settee, in which he sits

Cigar?
Arnold Thank you, no.
Henry (*sitting facing him*) The weather improves daily. Spring seems to
have come at last.

Arnold Quite. But really, Harnham, I can't stay long.

Henry I understand. You're probably wondering why I asked you to drop by.

Arnold Not really. I expected it. Sooner or later.

Henry (*coolly*) May I ask why?

Arnold Common sense, my dear Harnham. It was simply a matter of who sought out whom first.

Henry Look here, Slocombe, I'm not exactly on bended knee.

Arnold (*with easy courtesy*) Of course not. Such a posture would not suit you. I hold you in high esteem. You should know that.

Henry Yet I find you across my path wherever I go. Here in Salisbury. In Dorchester, Winchester, Weymouth. In short, everywhere I do business.

Arnold That's nothing personal. We are two wine merchants. I run my business, you run yours.

Henry I was in these places before you.

Arnold But my expansion is the greater.

Henry May I speak bluntly?

Arnold You are known for blunt speaking, Harnham.

Henry I consider your methods unfair.

Arnold In what way unfair?

Henry Pushy, I think. Somewhat vulgar, I fancy. The wine business is for gentlemen. Or was always considered so.

Arnold I have never been ashamed to call it a trade. But then, perhaps I'm no gentleman.

Henry These are nice distinctions. But not meaningless. I have the honour to be rather old-fashioned. I do not favour the new trends.

Arnold Times are changing. We have to go along with them.

Henry Come, Slocombe, it is ale that pleases the masses. Wine is for the discerning. The connoisseur. The gentry.

Arnold Didn't you miss something out?

Henry What?

Arnold The snob. Wine attracts snobs like a magnet. I would like to see it please the masses also.

Henry A forlorn hope in the long run. Though I grant you are making inroads.

Arnold So what do you want to discuss?

Henry I'll come to the point. Have you considered the advantages to both of us if our businesses were joined?

Arnold A merger?

Henry Whatever you choose to call it. In competition, our profits suffer from reduced prices. In partnership, the margins are restored. Think about it.

Arnold I have already done so.

Henry Then you agree we should not cut each other's throats?

Arnold It rather depends on who has the keener blade.

Henry At least you put your cards on the table. I admire that. But don't forget, Slocombe, that I know the business from long experience. Your cheap imports are a novelty. And novelties don't last.

Arnold Come, Harnham, my inroads are reaching your traditional end of the market also. Don't you forget that.

Henry Do I take it you oppose a merger on principle?

Arnold (*affably*) Oh, I have no firm principles in the matter. It's just that I have no complaint with things as they are. (*A pause*) Yet Slocombe and Harnham is not without a certain ring.

Henry (*silkily*) I was rather thinking of Harnham and Slocombe.

Arnold (*rising*) Frankly, Harnham, my business is on the way up. Any merger must recognize the facts. Think about *that*.

Henry At least we understand each other.

Arnold Why don't you come to dinner sometime? I'm sure there need be no animosity.

Edith enters with some papers

Edith I've brought the household accounts, Henry, as you asked me. (*She sees Arnold*) Oh, I'm sorry, I didn't know you had company.

Henry Edith, this is Arnold Slocombe. Slocombe—my wife, Edith.

Edith How do you do, Mr Slocombe.

Arnold Glad to know you, Mrs Harnham.

Edith They tell me your wine business is thriving.

Henry (*testily*) Yes, yes, Edith, that's enough. This is nothing to concern you.

Arnold (*to Edith*) We mustn't complain, as we say in the trade.

Henry (*patronizingly*) Run along now, my dear. You can bring those accounts later.

With a nod of acknowledgement at Arnold she goes

Arnold You have a most charming wife.

Henry She runs the house well.

Arnold And the business?

Henry (*stiffly*) Women have their world, we men have ours.

Arnold If ever I marry again, I hope my wife will belong to both.

Henry Ah, yes, you are a widower, I believe?

Arnold Not the happiest of conditions.

Henry No. A man needs a wife. One who is a credit to him. I have recently come across a case, affecting my own household, where that could not be said to apply.

Arnold Indeed?

Henry A rising gentleman. Married beneath him. It won't work.

Arnold (*politely*) I'm sorry to hear it. But now I really must go.

Henry (*pulling the bell*) The maid will see you out.

Arnold I'm glad we have had this exploratory talk. I shall bear in mind all you have said.

Betty, one of the housemaids, enters

Henry Betty, please show Mr Slocombe out.

Betty Yes, sir. Oh, sir?

Henry Yes, what is it?

Betty There's another gentleman just arrived. Name of Hardy. Here's his card, sir. (*She hands the card to Henry*)
Henry (*taking the card*) Did he state his business?
Betty No, sir. Said he's from Dorchester.
Henry Very well, I'll see him.

Arnold gives a brief bow and goes out with Betty

(*Placing the card on the desk*) Hardy, Hardy. I don't think I know a Mr Hardy.

Betty returns, followed by Thomas Hardy. In his early fifties, the novelist is every inch the man of affairs, alert, spry and confident of manner

Betty Mr Hardy, sir.
Henry Thank you, Betty.

She goes

Hardy Mr Henry Harnham?
Henry Yes. Please be seated, Mr Hardy.

Hardy sits on the settee

Now, What can I do for you, sir?
Hardy I come to you by recommendation. I am looking for a reliable wine merchant.
Henry I venture to say you have found one.
Hardy I keep establishments in Dorchester and London. My wife and I do a great deal of entertaining in both. It has been my misfortune to fall into the hands of cheats, sir. Penny-pinchers. Tradesmen in false labels. Adulterators, passing off inferior products.
Henry They are not unknown in the business.
Hardy I have a number of influential friends who are similarly placed. In the matter of wine, one cannot be too particular.
Henry (*warmly*) Indeed one cannot. If we are to talk business, sir, may I suggest we do so suitably refreshed?
Hardy By all means.
Henry (*pulling the bell*) If you would care to partake of a glass of Madeira, you will have some gauge of the quality of my products.
Hardy If I drink with you, sir, it is from conviviality, not to dispel doubt. You were recommended most highly.

Betty enters

Henry Betty, I want you to go down to the cellar and find a bottle of Maderia. The eighty-six vintage. Have it decanted and bring it here with two glasses.
Betty (*rushing off*) Yes, sir.
Henry Take your time. Don't hurry. More haste, less speed.
Betty Yes, sir.

She goes out, more slowly

Henry That girl is always rushing about. Directly she knows she has to fetch
something, she's like a scalded cat. (*He sighs*) Ah, domestic servants are
not what they were.

Hardy You think not?

Henry Though we did have an excellent one here. A girl named Anna. She
left to get married. But we were speaking of wine.

Hardy Yes.

Henry There is poetry in wine, sir. So many things to consider. Bouquet,
flavour, temperature. All so elusive. Then it must be matched with the
appropriate food. An excellent vintner's work is wasted if one has a bad
cook.

Hardy I believe you are a philosopher, sir.

Henry (*pleased, but modestly waving the remark away*) Then there's the soil.
One acre may yield ambrosial liquid, the adjoining one mere mouthwash.

Hardy Like the human race itself, eh?

Henry I'm not philosopher enough for that.

Hardy With people as with wine, we must cultivate the soil. Only by
studying the causes may we apply the effects. Is it any wonder the
scoundrels flourish? London is full of parvenus these days. As Mr Oscar
Wilde puts it, they know the price of everything and the value of nothing.
Such men are easy to fool.

Henry But not you, sir. A man of discernment. I knew it at once. May I
enquire what profession you pursue?

Hardy I am an architect, sir. Or was. Now somewhat retired from that
exacting occupation and dabbling in another in which mistakes may more
easily be made. I should like to entrust you with my business on a trial
basis of, shall we say six months?

Henry Excellent. My agent in Dorchester is a Mr Williams. I shall instruct
him to attend on you.

Hardy No need, my dear sir. I shall call on him myself this very afternoon.

Henry As you wish. I'll telephone him as soon as I have a moment.

Hardy Your house is very pleasantly situated, Mr Harnham.

Henry It answers well enough for my needs.

Hardy Almost in the shadow of the cathedral. Many centuries look down
on you, as Napoleon told his troops before the Battle of the Pyramids.

Henry These are lofty thoughts. My line, sir, consists in the rapid turnover
of merchandise.

Hardy Yes, you must keep your feet firmly planted on the ground. The
cathedral's turnover is the slow burning of faith.

Henry May I ask who recommended you to me?

Betty enters, carrying a tray on which are two glasses and a wine decanter

Hardy One Charles Bradford Raye. A barrister of Lincoln's Inn.

Betty, who is placing the drinks before them, reacts impulsively

Henry The deuce he did! Why, he married the very servant I mentioned just
now!

Betty Oh, sir, how is the gentleman?

Henry That will do, Betty.

Hardy No, please let me answer. (*To Betty*) He is in good health. I have a message for you also.

Betty For me, sir? Oh, sir!

Hardy For you are Betty, I see. Your former colleague, Mrs Raye, says she hopes you are well.

Betty Oh, yes, sir! Anything else?

Hardy Yes. Be careful of the fair when it visits.

Betty Oh, sir!

Henry That will be all, Betty.

Betty (*with a grateful glance at Hardy*) Yes, sir.

She exits

Hardy (*raising his glass*) Your good health.

Henry Yours.

They drink

Hardy An excellent Madeira. It fully confirms the recommendation.

Henry Thank you.

Hardy I hope I did not speak out of turn to your servant.

Henry It is not for me to criticize London ways. For myself, I believe domestic servants should be kept in their place.

Hardy An interesting point. It concerns the very people of whom we have just been speaking.

Henry Yes. I see you know Anna already.

Hardy Yes. Does she not show that a servant's place is not something fixed by the Almighty? It can change. People sometimes go up, sometimes down. Like that hobby-horse on which the young lady was riding when she first met her future husband.

Henry You know the history, then?

Hardy I do. As told to me, it seemed to have all the ingredients of a bitter-sweet story. If only one could find the missing piece of the jigsaw.

Henry How did you meet these people?

Hardy My wife and I were invited to a dinner party in Lincoln's Inn. Our host was an elderly circuit judge, a widower who has an excellent cook/housekeeper. The gathering was of a mainly legal character. Mr Raye and another barrister, their wives, a lawyer's clerk, and Miss Charlotte Raye.

Henry Oh, yes, I've heard of her.

Hardy A formidable lady. I understand she has been in correspondence with your wife since the two young persons were married.

Henry Very likely. My wife scribbles endlessly. It helps her pass the time.

Hardy At dinner, I observed Anna Raye. So eager to please, but so unsuited to the occasion. She seemed unsure which knives and forks to use for different courses. Her husband prompted her, but everyone noticed.

Henry I knew it all along. An excellent servant makes a bad mistress.

Hardy When asked to taste a newly opened bottle of wine, she complained that it was sour.

Henry Good Lord!

Hardy She expressed herself with refreshing vigour. The wine was of a most superior vintage. The judge dealt with her *faux pas* with a teasing courtesy. "I suppose, Mrs Raye, we shall all have to martyr ourselves." And as he sipped, he smacked his lips with obvious relish.

Henry And then?

Hardy Every time she tried to contribute to the conversation, her husband cut her short. In the end, she retired with a headache.

Henry That marriage was a calamity. I said it from the beginning.

Hardy Yes, but how could it have happened? That was the missing piece of the jigsaw. The when and where are easy. It is the how that makes the story. I studied Charles Raye from close quarters. He was quick, alert, intelligent. Just the man to go far in his profession. And she? Pretty and decorative. Nothing more. Like the picture on a chocolate box.

Henry And now he's stuck with her.

Hardy And stuck in the lower reaches of his profession, in all probability.

Henry He has only himself to blame.

Hardy I wonder. Are we not all pawns of fate, Mr Harnham?

Henry I can't afford to be anyone's pawn. I built up a business with the sweat of my brow. If the bank lent me money, it wasn't because they liked the look of my face. They saw me as a good risk. Anyone could see that Anna was a bad risk.

Hardy Matrimonially, you mean?

Henry For a professional man, most certainly. (*A pause*) For the driver of the dogcart, no doubt she would have made a splendid match.

Edith enters with some papers

Edith Oh, dear, this is not my lucky morning.

Henry Edith, this is Mr Hardy. An architect from London. He is acquainted with the Rayes.

Edith Oh. (*She extends her hand*) How do you do, Mr Hardy. Do you bring news of Anna?

Hardy (*rising*) I do indeed.

Henry Well, you must tell my wife about it. This seems a good opportunity for me to contact my agent in Dorchester. We'll look at those accounts later. (*He takes them*) You will excuse me? (*He starts to go*)

Hardy Of course.

Henry (*turning back*) Edith, you must ask Mr Hardy to tell you about a missing piece of some jigsaw puzzle.

Henry exits

Edith sits, and Hardy resumes his place on the settee

Edith A missing piece? What jigsaw puzzle?

Hardy Mrs Harnham, I can't tell you how delighted I am to meet you. For you are part of it.

Edith Have we met before?

Hardy Never, to the best of my knowledge.

Edith There seems something familiar about your features.

Hardy (*smiling*) They are not entirely unknown.

Edith I certainly don't recall meeting any architects from London.

Hardy London and Dorchester. But your husband is a little out of date. I abandoned the profession some years ago for the trade of writing.

Edith How modest you are, to abandon a profession for a trade.

Hardy My name is Thomas Hardy.

Edith Of course. The famous author. I should have guessed. I have just been reading a novel of yours, Mr Hardy. *The Mayor of Casterbridge*. I liked it immensely.

Hardy How kind of you to say so.

Edith I am intrigued by your way of disguising things. Of superimposing your invented world on the real one. Casterbridge is your native Dorchester. Then why not say so?

Hardy Because it is the Dorchester of my perception only. All its citizens carry their own Dorchester in their heads. Casterbridge happens to be mine.

Edith Your jigsaw puzzle no longer surprises me.

Hardy It concerns Anna and Charles Raye. Having met you, I feel sure you will be able to supply the missing piece.

Edith I do have my secrets, you know.

Hardy Of course. But a writer is a kind of licensed vagabond. I met the Rayes at the house of a judge. The puzzle is his marriage to Anna.

Edith And the missing piece, I suppose, is how it came about?

Hardy How well you understand. You know Miss Charlotte Raye, I believe?

Edith We have not met. I wrote to her on the girl's behalf. She sent me a graceful letter in return.

Hardy (*nodding*) On the girl's behalf ... precisely.

Edith Precisely what, Mr Hardy?

Hardy I questioned Miss Charlotte closely. She gave little away, beyond saying her brother had wooed Anna by correspondence. And yet you wrote to her on Anna's behalf. Was she too busy to write?

Edith (*hesitating*) No, not exactly.

Hardy Not at all, I believe.

Edith You were not out of place in that judge's house. I think you would have made a first-rate lawyer yourself.

Hardy Then what I suspect is true?

Edith I would never survive your cross-examination for five minutes. Yes, I wrote her letters for her. At the time, I thought I could not very well refuse. Now, I am not so sure. The road to hell is paved with good intentions. My old governess taught me all the proverbs. When I married my husband——

Hardy (*sharply*) Yes?

Edith It will not have escaped your notice that he is, well, old enough to be my father.

Hardy You are an extremely attractive woman.

Edith The lawyer's trick of antithesis. Creating a damaging impression.

Hardy I was not aware I did so.

Edith You implied it. Shall I supply the words, Mr Hardy? "You are an extremely attractive woman. While your husband is old and grey and very dull."

Hardy (*smiling*) No such thing. Old? Heavens, I myself could probably give him a year or two. Grey? What of that? Some men are grey at thirty. As to the dullness, only you can be the judge of that.

Edith Well, I've said enough on that subject.

Hardy I might add that I also questioned Charles Raye.

Edith I'm not surprised.

Hardy It was he who suggested I call here.

Edith For what purpose?

Hardy Ostensibly, to discuss business with your husband. Oh it's all quite legitimate. I was looking to change my wine merchant.

Edith How very convenient.

Hardy Convenient?

Edith Useful, I meant. That my husband happened to be in that line of business.

Hardy I think you meant convenient as well, Mrs Harnham. Charles Raye certainly did. Though he only hinted at it, he seemed anxious for me to see you.

Edith I can't imagine why. That young man and I said goodbye for ever some weeks ago.

Hardy So he told me. Yet there seemed something half-hearted about the phrase. For ever is a long time. I had the impression he would like to shorten it somewhat.

Edith How do you know?

Hardy Mrs Harnham, we are strangers. And strangers are supposed to confine their conversation to polite generalities. May I take the licence of a vagabond and speak more freely?

Edith Go on.

Hardy Our mutual friend has embroiled himself in a marriage which seems certain to blight his career. As things stand.

Edith As things stand?

Hardy There is a potential remedy.

Edith Is there? Anna is a girl with no social graces and little education. She is expecting a child. Together, the facts make up a grim equation.

Hardy Even grimmer, if we take a third fact into account.

Edith Which is?

Hardy Charles Raye is in love with you.

Edith (*turning away*) Oh, come!

Hardy I read it in his eyes, and in the eagerness he betrayed whenever your name was mentioned. Now you confirm the truth about the letters, the picture is complete.

Edith That is one of life's little ironies.

Hardy I like the phrase. In such a situation, some sacrifices have to be made by—well, by someone. May I ask you a very personal question, Mrs Harnham? Of course you need not answer it.

Edith Well?

Hardy Are you in love with Charles Raye?

Edith (*casting her eyes down*) Thank you for giving me the option. I prefer not to answer.

Hardy I think you have just done so.

Edith The sacrifices you speak of have already been made.

Hardy Yet there is another, which might lead to a happier outcome.

Edith Another?

Hardy The impression I formed of Anna was not unfavourable. She will never amount to much, perhaps. But if I am not mistaken, she is a vessel into which much may be poured.

Edith Perhaps. With the help of a strong and trusted tutor.

Hardy She is malleable, and bright enough. She will never learn originality of thought. But what of that? Few people possess it.

Edith I take your point.

Hardy But the world judges from the surface. What she *can* do is acquire a passable accent and enough social fluency to be a useful wife to an ambitious barrister. Why, many a Lord Chancellor's wife has been made from less promising material.

Edith But who is to teach her?

Hardy You, Mrs Harnham.

Edith I?

Hardy That would be the most fitting sacrifice of all. (*A pause*) Since you yourself were in a measure responsible.

She remains silent

I've offended you. Forgive my presumption.

Edith Offended? No, no. But of course the whole idea is unthinkable.

Hardy Then consider the alternative. A career needlessly wrecked. Two lives made miserable. And all for the sake of a few letters, kindly meant and kindly sent. (*He shrugs*) But such things have happened before, and I daresay will happen again.

Edith Did Miss Raye put you up to this?

Hardy Not at all. But I have said too much. Thank you for filling in that missing piece.

Edith (*with a wan smile*) Is this how a vagabond usually behaves? Unsettling people's minds?

Hardy Forgive me. I see I've caused you some distress.

Edith (*thinking aloud*) It's true I have time on my hands. And the child is not due for several months. And I do have something to atone for. Much may be done in that time. The groundwork, at least. And I do lack an occupation.

Hardy The same may be said of many married women. It was the curse of our society. So much of our natural resources going to waste. (*He looks up as . . .*)

Henry enters

Ah, Mr Harnham.

Henry I hope you have not been bored, Mr Hardy.

Hardy Not a bit. We have been having a most interesting discussion.

Henry I have spoken to Mr Williams. For once in a way, the telephone worked. A wonderful invention, though I doubt it will ever be a reliable means of communication.

Hardy I'm much obliged to you.

Henry Here is his card. He will expect you this afternoon. (*He hands a card to Hardy*) Of course, you are most welcome to stay for lunch.

Hardy Some other time, perhaps. We both have much to see to, Mrs Harnham.

Edith Yes.

Hary I bid you both a good-day. I'll see myself out, Mr Harnham

Hardy exits

Henry watches him going, thoughtfully

Henry What did he mean by saying you have much to see to?

Edith We were talking of Anna.

Henry But she no longer concerns you.

Edith So *I* thought, until a few minutes ago. Mr Hardy is a very persuasive man.

Henry I believe the connection can be most valuable.

Edith What connection?

Henry The business, my dear, of course.

Edith (*busy with her own thoughts*) Oh, that!

Henry If I mistake not, our Mr Hardy is a man of some influence.

Edith Yes, I believe he is.

Henry A man who entertains. A man whose friends entertain. I fancy he will prove no ordinary customer. (*He chuckles*) What price Slocombe and Harnham now? When I started out in this business, I soon learned the importance of spreading the word. A customer satisfied is a customer who spreads the word. And one recommendation leads to another.

Edith Henry, I have it in mind to take Anna back into the fold. For a little while.

Henry Good heavens, is her husband divorcing her?

Edith Not that I know of.

Henry Then I can only conclude you mean to abduct her.

Edith Not at all. Take her off her husband's hands. I mean to give her a little polish. In return for her services.

Henry (*suspiciously*) The architect is behind all this.

Edith (*with ironical emphasis*) The *architect* could be useful in building up your business.

Henry True, true.

Edith Besides, I am bored, and often at a loose end. It will occupy my time.

Henry There is that, of course. When do you mean to start?

Edith As soon as possible. I shall write to Miss Charlotte Raye.

Henry (*won over*) Well, I daresay you could use a reliable personal maid.

Edith She will be a companion, not a domestic.

Henry I don't hold with your modern ideas. Would you try to educate her above her station?

Edith Have you forgotten what her new station is?
Henry A false one, I'll be bound.
Edith (*sitting at the desk*) Please ring for Betty.
Henry As you wish.

Edith begins to write as Henry rings. She doesn't look up as he leaves

Henry leaves. Presently Betty enters

Betty You rang, madam?
Edith (*still writing*) I intend to ask Anna down to stay for a while.
Betty But she's a married woman now.
Edith The fact had not escaped me. If she comes, I want you to have her old room prepared for her.
Betty You don't mean to have her back in service, madam?
Edith It is I who will be in service. She is to be my companion. As a mother-to-be, her work will be mental, not physical.
Betty (*bridling*) Does that mean she'll be over me?
Edith Not at all. (*She puts the letter in an envelope, stamps and seals it*) In any case, perhaps she won't come.
Betty She was always very fond of you, madam.
Edith And I of her, Betty. And now, will you please tidy up in here?
Betty Right away, madam. (*She begins to arrange cushions and tidy the room*)

Edith goes, taking the letter

That Anna. She'll be quite hoity-toity now. Allus did have the mistress round her little finger. (*She picks up the card which has been lying on the desk*) Mr Thomas Hardy. Nice gentleman. Bet he has a story or two to tell.

CURTAIN

SCENE 3

The same. Early evening, several days later

Edith, evidently expecting somebody, is plumping cushions, making small adjustments to ornaments etc.

Betty enters in her usual fluster

Betty There's a lady come to see you, madam.
Edith Well, Betty?
Betty Shall I ask her to come in?
Edith I suppose she has a name?
Betty Oh, madam, yes, how silly of me, I forgot. Miss Charlotte Raye.
Edith Yes. Show her in, will you?
Betty (*at the door*) Oh, madam?

Edith Yes?

Betty Would that be Anna's new sister-in-law?

Edith It would, as a matter of fact.

Betty Thought it would. (*Calling from the door*). Madam says you're to come in.

Edith (*reproving but kindly*) Betty, how many times must I tell you not to act like a fairground barker? You must show visitors in properly. Otherwise, what will they think of the manners in this house?

Charlotte enters briskly, like a whirlwind. She is a woman of about Edith's age, perhaps a year or two older, full of energy and with an overpowering personality

Charlotte This one doesn't give a fig! (*She sweeps across the room, hand outstretched*) Charlotte Raye's the name. Mrs Edith Harnham, I presume?

Edith, after shaking hands, withdraws from what has evidently been an uncommonly hearty grip

Edith How kind of you to come all this way, Miss Raye.

Charlotte Call me Charlotte, because I intend to call you Edith.

Betty is gawping, unwilling to leave

And this is the excellent Betty, I suppose? Well, Betty, I'm sure your mistress is about to ask me if I'd like a cup of tea. And since the answer is "yes", I might as well save her the trouble.

Edith (*overcome*) Won't you have a cup of tea ... Charlotte?

Charlotte I do believe I will. Off you go, girl. Here's sixpence. For taking my coat so nicely. (*She hands Betty a coin*)

Betty (*gratefully taking it*) Oh, thanks ever so, madam.

Charlotte (*clapping her hands*) Shoo! Shoo!

Betty Won't be long, madam. There's some already brewing.

Betty goes out backwards with an awed look

Charlotte sits on the settee

Edith Please be seated.

Charlotte (*appreciating the humour*) Thank you. (*She rises, dusts the seat and sits down again*) Afraid I never was much of a one for the formalities. Not if the atmosphere is right. Which it is. Felt it as soon as I came in. Now if your husband had received me, I would have followed the polite forms to the letter. The meaningless courtesies. Do you follow me?

Edith I follow you. And now, what news of Anna?

Charlotte Ah, dear, tiresome little Anna. I feel a sense of guilt in this affair, you know.

Edith Why should you?

Charlotte Because I'm a frightful busybody. We unmarried Rayes were always a meddlesome breed.

Edith I thought I was the one who did the meddling. Tell me more.

Charlotte In the matter of the letters. I should have guessed the truth. I did not. I advised Charles wrongly. Just how wrongly I have only lately discovered.

Edith What do you mean?

Charlotte (*holding up her hand, like a teacher rebuking her pupil*) All in good time. Charles is an impulsive soul, as you may have gathered. Shrewd in matters affecting his profession. But very gullible. I had not met the girl, else my advice would have been very different. But what right did I have to advise him, *not* having met her?

Edith That's all water under the bridge. What are we to do next? That's the question.

Charlotte As I learn from your letter, you have met Mr Hardy.

Edith Yes.

Charlotte Another meddler, or my name's not Charlotte Raye.

Edith I admire his forthrightness. He wanted to help.

Charlotte Don't we all? He has an inquisitive mind. He wants to control the game. To write the story. And so he made you promise to take Anna under your wing.

Edith He only *suggested* it. And he was right to do so. I feel *responsible*.

Charlotte Yes, I do see your point.

Edith If Anna is to bear Charles' child . . .

Betty enters with a tray of tea-things

Betty Here's the tea, madam.

Edith Thank you, Betty. Just put it down, will you? I'll pour.

Betty (*putting the tray on the small table*) Yes, madam. Will that be all? (*She hopes it won't*)

Edith (*firmly*) Yes, Betty.

Betty leaves, quite slowly

Charlotte (*rising, anticipating Edith*) Allow me. (*She pours tea and hands a cup to Edith*)

Edith Thank you.

Charlotte (*sitting, sipping tea*) For all his wisdom, Mr Hardy is not quite up-to-date. Someone else is writing the story.

Edith What do you mean?

Charlotte There is to be no child.

Edith No child! (*She rises, agitated*) I—I don't understand.

Charlotte Sit down, Edith. Be patient. Compose yourself.

Edith sits

That's better. Now. Some days ago, the girl was in pain, and took to her bed. Charles called me. I have done some nursing, you know.

Edith Yes, I thought you might have done.

Charlotte She made a complete recovery. There will be no baby.

Edith You mean she miscarried?

Charlotte There was nothing to miscarry.

Edith I'm out of my depth.

Charlotte It was an overblown fantasy, if I may so express it. A phantom pregnancy. She was never with child.

Edith Is such a thing possible?

Charlotte Oh, yes. It was self-induced.

Edith Self-induced?

Charlotte Our Anna is in good company. Mary Tudor had a phantom pregnancy. Medical science cannot explain it. Perhaps it will one day. Have you heard of the unconscious mind?

Edith No.

Charlotte An eminent doctor in Vienna has proposed the theory. One Sigmund Freud. I suggest the case of Anna gives it substance. She *wanted* to believe she was with child. More important, she wanted Charles to believe it. And so she made it happen. But as a fiction, not a fact.

Edith So all that ties the two together now is the marriage bond.

Charlotte All? It's a powerful enough tie. Or so the world understands.

Edith And what do *you* understand, Charlotte?

Charlotte rises. During the following scene she is on her feet, active and restless, using the full area of the stage to prowl around

Charlotte I? That Charles fell out of love with her as quickly as he fell in. And that he is now in love with—(*she swings round and fixes her gaze on Edith*)—shall I say someone else?

Edith What am I to do, Charlotte?

Charlotte Why do people always look to us spinsters for advice? Mine could be dangerous.

Edith Sometimes I think my life isn't dangerous enough. The likes of me aren't cut out for danger.

Charlotte And just what sort of people are the likes of you, Edith?

Edith Charming hostesses, kept on leashes. Cultivated persons. Women whose mission is to please their husbands. What sort of dangerous advice would you have to offer, Charlotte?

Charlotte I don't believe in leashes. Except for pets.

Edith You are a remarkable woman.

Charlotte (*in full spate; moving freely*) Stuff and nonsense! This is supposed to be an age of enlightenment. It is an age of hypocrisy. Of noble sentiments and empty deeds. Men control the strings, and women dance to their tune. It's time we took a stand!

Edith I'm sure you're right.

Charlotte Of course I'm right. Men who betray their wives are admired. Women who betray their husbands are social pariahs. And why should these things be so, you ask.

Edith Did I?

Charlotte I'll tell you.

Edith I thought you would.

Charlotte Through custom, nothing but custom. Not by divine edict. Oh, no. No thunderbolt would fall from heaven if these things were altered. So why are they not altered?

Edith Custom?

Charlotte Exactly. Custom. The deadliest of vices. There is no outrage, not one, which custom cannot make into the norm.

Edith None?

Charlotte None. Take war. The greatest pestilence of the race. Men slaughter for a flag, and are heroes. Widows grieve, and are unheeded. The greater the butchery, the bigger the celebration. Take slavery. Tolerated for centuries, as if it were in the natural order. In some parts of the world, cannibalism is an honoured practice. In others, infanticide. And all in the name of custom.

Edith At least we are comparatively civilized.

Charlotte Are we? Women are willing drudges. Can you deny it?

Edith What we need is the vote.

Charlotte (*snorting in derision*) Votes are the *illusion* of power, not power itself. One day all women will have the vote. And it will change nothing. One gang replaces another. If the votes really changed society, they would be made illegal at once.

Edith Charlotte, weren't you going to give me some advice?

Charlotte I stand rebuked. (*She resumes her seat*) Why didn't you stop me before?

Edith I was interested. I think you've opened my eyes a little.

Charlotte Why did you marry, Edith?

Edith Cowardice, I suppose. I chose the safe life.

Charlotte And now you mean to educate your former servant to become a fit wife for the man you love. You do love him, Edith, don't you?

Edith Stop! You are confusing me.

Charlotte Look out of the window.

Edith The window?

Charlotte Do as I say!

Responding to Charlotte's peremptory tone of command, Edith goes to the window and looks out. She gives a convulsive start

Edith Charles!

Charlotte Yes. Do you wish to see him, Edith?

Edith Why have you done this to me?

Charlotte Come, Edith, let's not be naïve. I came here to Salisbury, at your invitation. I happened to be chaperoned by my brother. It's up to you to decide whether you want to see him.

Edith (*after a painful pause, quietly*) You have gone to much trouble. How can I refuse?

Charlotte Very well. (*She goes to the window, looks out and makes a sign*) He has seen me.

Edith (*nervously*) This is really too absurd. Is he coming?

Charlotte Life is absurd, is it not? He is coming.

Edith (*excited, with the eagerness of a schoolgirl*) Marvellously, ridiculously absurd. And you most absurd of all.

Charlotte On the contrary, I am an apostle of the obvious.

Edith (*in a flutter, patting her hair*) Do I look all right?

Charlotte You would, if you'd stop fiddling with your hair. Compose yourself.

Betty rushes in at the double, in a state of suppressed excitement

Betty (*to Edith*) Oh, madam, what do you think? Mr Raye's here.

Edith Then you'd better show him in. And remember what I told you about announcing visitors.

Betty Yes, madam.

Betty withdraws, then enters with exaggerated dignity to admit Charles

Mr Charles Raye.

Edith (*striving to appear calm*) How kind of you to call, Mr Raye. I hope you bring good news of your wife.

Charles (*gravely*) She sends you greetings.

Charlotte And now I must be about my business. My coat, Betty.

Betty (*bustling again*) Right away, madam.

Betty exits briskly

Edith (*nervously, to Charlotte*) You aren't going?

Charlotte I must.

Edith Won't you stay a little longer?

Charlotte If you need me, I am lodging at the *County Arms*.

Charlotte exits

Edith Oh. She's gone.

Charles (*smiling*) So I see.

An embarrassed pause

Edith Well, Mr Raye?

Charles Well, Mrs Harnham?

Edith Your sister has explained my proposal concerning Anna?

Charles At some length.

Edith She is a lady who leaves no "i" undotted.

Charles Nor any "t" uncrossed.

Edith No ground untraversed.

Charles No stone unturned.

They both begin to laugh at themselves. It breaks the ice

Edith May I call you Charles?

Charles Like you did on the day of my marriage?

Edith Like I did on the day you said we would never meet again.

Charles I thought we never would.

Edith Do you still have my letters?

Charles How could I destroy such gems?

Edith You said you would.

Charles A rash resolve. I shall treasure them always. When I sit at the table and see the honest, simple, trusting features of my wife, I think of those letters and smile. She looks at me, and thinks the smile is for her. And so happiness is parcelled out, with just enough to go round. One smile does double duty.

Edith You are taking this very philosophically.

Charles How else should I take it?

Edith Then you are a fatalist?

Charles A lawyer cannot afford to be that. When driven into a corner, he must find a way out.

Edith I never meant to drive you into a corner.

Charles A good advocate makes the best of a bad brief.

Edith Poor Charles. Has she let you down *very* badly?

Charles She has been herself, that's all.

Edith And the false pregnancy?

Charles If doctors do not understand these things, how should a mere lawyer?

Edith Did it come as a blow to you?

Charles Not at all. It came as a relief. Since there was no life to lose in the first place, it follows that no pain was inflicted. I can look to the future with a clearer eye.

Edith The future, yes. I made Mr Hardy a promise. I mean to keep it. Perhaps I can complete his story for him.

Charles You are freed from any obligation, Edith.

Edith Child or no child, you are chained to Anna. You have a great future, Charles. Heaven forbid that Anna should spoil it.

Charles (*with wonder*) You would make such a sacrifice ... for me?

Edith Sacrifice? I am an idle woman. My husband expects it. He's the active one. Making money, expanding his little empire. He means to be the biggest wine merchant in the region. (*After a pause, with feeling*) And I sit here at home ... doing the household accounts.

Charles How bitter you sound.

Edith Anna is my challenge. Once I wrote her letters for her, and earned her the love of a fine young man. Now I shall make a proper wife of her, and earn her his respect.

Charles It was a phantom love. Like the pregnancy.

Edith No more?

Charles Or a love misdirected. (*A pause*) A love meant for another.

As their words become more and more charged with intimacy, they are also moving closer together in point of physical distance

Edith For one, perhaps, who took it all too much to heart.

Charles It was yourself you poured into those letters.

Edith A woman must be allowed her mistakes.

Charles It was no mistake, Edith.

Edith (*struggling to convince herself*) It *has* to be a mistake. We can never mean anything to each other.

Charles Never?

Edith Take care, Charles.

Charles My sister has taught me to be bold. To strike out at convention. I owe Anna nothing. (*Vehemently*) Nothing, do you hear? She won me under false colours. If you reject me, at least do so under true ones, not as a slave to convention.

Edith This is dangerous talk. It's my duty to stop it here and now.

Charles (*drawing away; speaking without looking at her*) I shall not reproach you if you do. The subject will not be mentioned again.

Edith Charles. Look at me.

He turns

You kissed me . . . on your wedding-day.

Charles I only claimed the price for your letters.

Edith It was a fair price.

Charles Yet I gave you a choice. Your cheek or your lips.

Edith And I made it.

Charles (*closer*) You loved me.

Edith Yes.

Charles You love me still.

Edith It doesn't help.

Charles And your husband means nothing to you.

Edith When Anna told me she was expecting a baby, I had a dreadful wish.

Charles What was it?

Edith That the child were mine.

Charles (*touching her hand*) Was it so dreadful?

Edith Your sister would not say so.

Charles I asked you, not my sister.

Edith Not all of us find it so easy to strike out at convention.

Charles What she thinks today, perhaps the world will think tomorrow.

Edith Do you think so? (*Fervently*) Oh, Charles, do you really think so?

Charles Let me ask you a delicate question.

Edith Well?

Charles Your husband. Is he a husband in the . . . *fullest* sense?

Edith (*confused*) Well, I—I—I don't quite know what to say.

Charles Tell me to mind my own business.

Edith I'm afraid it *is* your business.

Charles Well, then?

Edith He comes to my bed occasionally.

He turns away as if struck by a blow

He *is* my lawful husband, after all.

Charles (*facing her*) I had no right to turn away.

Edith To put your mind at rest, what happens is more in his head than anywhere else. Do you understand?

Charles (*softly*) Yes.

Edith His performance is, well, like Anna with her baby. (*Plunging on with a kind of desperation*) Charles, I might as well tell you all. I can't stop now. There is a shadow between us.

Charles A shadow?

Edith He wants a child. So badly. And nothing happens. Being a man, he is convinced the fault is mine.

Charles I see. (*With restrained bitterness*) So *that's* why you wished the child were yours.

Edith Yes. No. Oh, Charles, I'm so confused. So capable in some things, so inadequate in this. (*Urgently*) Don't you see? I wanted it to be *yours* as well. Now do you see? Do you?

Charles (*radiant*) Oh, *darling* Edith. There is a remedy.

Edith No, Charles, no!

Charles I shall not be in these parts again for some time. If you still wish to coach Anna, I shall send for her tomorrow. And in the meantime . . .

Edith Yes?

Charles I'm staying at the *County Arms*.

Edith (*urgently*) Charles, you must go now!

Charles Where is your husband?

Edith In Dorchester. He returns tomorrow.

Charles Tomorrow!

Edith Charles, I can read your thoughts. You must not think them.

Charles It's now or never.

Edith (*with regret, but half-heartedly*) Then it must be never.

Charles (*towards the door*) I must go to my sister now.

Edith (*anguished*) Charles, I . . .

Charles (*looking at her fixedly*) To the *County Arms*. If you meant what you said, you will join me there later.

Edith You know it's out of the question!

Charles Is it?

Edith The risk. Think of the risk.

Charles Is it so great? (*Coolly*) My sister is with me, remember.

Edith Go, Charles—for God's sake, go!

Charles If you fail to come, then all is over between us. This time for good. I shall never reproach you. Never. Is it goodbye, Edith? Or au revoir?

He turns on his heels. His hand is on the door

Edith Charles?

Charles (*turning*) Yes?

Edith If I'm not there by nine o'clock, do not expect me.

Charles (*with a slight smile*) Thank you, Edith.

Charles exits

Edith Oh, heavens, what shall I do? What *shall* I do? (*She paces up and down in great agitation*) Now or never. So cool he is, with his legal brain.

Betty enters

Betty Oh, madam, Mr Raye left just now. In such a hurry he was, too.

Edith looks at Betty standing there, all flutter and excitement, and suddenly becomes very calm herself. She has reached her decision, and speaks with quiet resolution

Edith Yes, Betty, I know. His sister was expecting him. I have arranged to

rejoin them later at the *County Arms*. To discuss the arrival of Anna, you
know. She will be here tomorrow.

Betty Yes, madam.

Edith (*on her full dignity*) I may be rather late. You need not wait up.

CURTAIN

SCENE 4

The same. The following afternoon

*Betty and Anna enter. The latter is smartly dressed and preening herself, much
to Betty's wonder and delight.*

Betty Let's have a good look at you, then.

Anna poses like a mannequin

Lor, Anna, is it really you?

Anna Like the suit, do you? 'Fraid it's mussed-up from travelling.

Betty You look a real lady.

Anna Married woman's good enough for me.

Betty How long is it now?

Anna Two months and three days.

Betty What happened to the baby, Anna? I heard stories.

Anna (*sharply*) What stories? Someone been talking out of turn?

Betty Only that you'd lost it. Don't get shirty, Anna.

Anna Sorry, Betty. Yes, I did lose it, and that's a fact. It hit me real bad.
Like to hear about it?

Betty Oh, yes.

Anna Well, you've heard of them, what do you call, miscarriages?

Betty Yes.

Anna The pain was something chronic. And next thing I knew, it was gone,
and—oh, Betty, I dunno as I'll ever be able to have a baby now.

Betty Go on, never say die. (*She puts her hand to her mouth*) Oops, sorry, I
didn't mean ...

Anna 'S all right, you can say it. We're friends.

Betty Never mind, you've still got Charles. Proper good-looker he is.

Anna He is and all. I'd kill him if he ever looked at another woman.

Betty Quite right. (*A pause*) Think he will?

Anna Not if I know my Charles. He loves me.

Betty And so he should. Why wouldn't he?

Anna But why's he not here? He sent for me.

Betty Didn't he meet you off the train, then?

Anna (*airily*) Oh, I missed the one I should've been on. Didn't I tell you?

Betty You *missed* it?

Anna What if I did? Woman's privilege. There was two close together. He
should've waited till the next one. But not him. (*Resentfully*) And now
he's not even here to meet me.

Betty You want a lot, don't you?

Anna What are husbands for but to wait on their wives?

Betty (*giggling*) Proper little madam you are, and that's a fact.

Anna Didn't even say why he wanted me down. What's all this about, Betty?

Betty You'll find out soon enough.

Anna You mean you know?

Betty (*mysteriously*) Maybe I do and maybe I don't.

Anna What's that supposed to mean when it's at home? Come to think of it, where's the mistress?

Betty Dunno. Haven't seen her since last night. Prob'ly down to the *County Arms* with your husband and his sister.

Anna Well, they'll turn up soon, I 'spect. Let's you and me go down to the parlour for a cup of tea. You can tell me what's been happening since I went away.

Betty Right you are.

They leave, chattering away merrily. After a few moments Charles, Charlotte and Edith enter

Charlotte That girl needs her bottom spanked.

Charles Don't worry. No doubt she missed the train. There was another one close behind.

Charlotte If you're in such a forgiving mood, why didn't you meet that one as well?

Charles There are limits, Charlotte. I'm not at her beck and call. She knows her way here well enough.

Charlotte And her luggage?

Charles She can leave it at the station. I'll collect it later.

Edith Then you've already trained her in the practical things?

Charles Oh, she's not a fool.

Charlotte But is Betty? That's the question. You stayed out all night, Edith.

Edith (*happily*) I know. Dreadful, isn't it? (*She does a little pirouette*) Why don't I feel dreadful? Tell me that, you wonderfully absurd woman.

Charles Edith, you really must *try* to feel dreadful.

Edith Nonsense. What price convention now? (*She impulsively hugs him*) There.

Charles Edith, careful!

Edith (*releasing him*) Cowardy custard! (*Gaily*) I've decided to whisk your wife off to Europe.

Charles (*amazed*) You've decided *what*?

Charlotte Look here, Edith, this is going too far. A fortnight in Salisbury was what we had in mind.

Charles If that. Can't you see how last night changes things? For you, of all people, to feel obligations to Anna!

Edith It's I of all people who should. Remember what you said yesterday, Charlotte? About Mr Hardy wanting to write the story? Well, my compliments to the famous author, but I'll write my own, if it's all the same to him. Charles, I'll bring you home a real wife. A groundwork in

Italian, perhaps a little French. At least enough phrases for an elderly circuit judge. A smattering of history, the rudiments of polite society.

Charlotte I seem to have opened the bottle and let out a genie.

Charles But why, Edith, why?

Edith (*in mock surprise at the silliness of the question*) Because I have no career of my own, so I choose to work for yours.

Charlotte Now who's a wonderfully absurd woman?

Henry enters

Henry Edith, where have you been? I've been looking all over for you. Ah. Miss Raye, Mr Raye, how do you do.

Edith How long have you been back?

Henry Oh, about half an hour. Why do you ask?

Edith (*suppressing her relief*) I was looking for *you* earlier. To tell you I was off to the *County Arms* to pick up our visitors.

Henry Ah, that explains it.

Anna enters

Edith Anna, my dear! Have you been playing hide and seek?

Anna I caught the second train. Charles, why didn't you meet me?

Charles (*coolly*) I met the first one.

Henry So, Anna, my wife intends to ask you to stay with us for a while.

Charlotte It seems she has more ambitious plans. Tell her, Edith.

Edith How would you like to come with me to the Continent, Anna?

Anna The *Continent*! Oh, lor!

Henry (*sharply*) What's that?

Edith Henry, perhaps we can discuss this in private.

Henry (*grimly*) I think we'd better. (*To the Rayes*) Excuse my bewilderment. It seems I am no longer privy to my wife's plans.

Edith Well, Anna, what do you say?

Anna (*excitedly*) It's the chance of a lifetime! But what do *you* say, Charles?

Charles What *can* I say? Mrs Harnham has quite a way with her.

Edith Then that's settled. Off you go now, all of you.

Charles gives a helpless, disclaiming shrug of the shoulders as he leaves with Anna. Charlotte follows, shaking her head

Henry Well, Edith, I'm waiting for an explanation.

Edith (*in a conciliatory mood*) Henry, you've been telling me for some time I need a change.

Henry A change, yes: but this! Do you think I'm made of money?

Edith Remember I have some of my own.

Henry (*changing his tune*) I see. And you intend to use that?

Edith You know I wouldn't dream of asking you to finance a whim of mine. I feel responsible for Anna. If I don't make at least half a lady of her, it will not be for the want of trying.

Henry Well, perhaps I was a little hasty. I may say I have just concluded some useful business in Dorchester. Thanks to Mr Hardy. (*He bangs his fist in his palm*) Damn it, Edith, you *shall* go to the Continent with Anna.

The change will do you a world of good. And I shall provide—(*he hesitates a moment*)—well, at least your basic expenses. Any fripperies will of course be your own affair.

Edith Of course.

Henry And how long do you mean to stay?

Edith I haven't decided. I only made up my mind just now to go at all. But before I leave, I want to come to a better understanding with you.

Henry (*suspiciously*) What is it you want of me?

Edith Nothing, Henry. How suspicious you are. All I meant was that you and I—(*coyly wheedling*)—have not been all we should to each other.

Henry And whose fault is that?

Edith Let us not speak of fault. You have not come to my room lately.

Henry You have hardly encouraged me.

Edith Let bygones be bygones. I'm encouraging you now.

Henry's face suddenly lights up. The years fall away, and he is a young man again, with a young man's ardour. He takes both her hands in his and looks lovingly into her eyes

Henry Oh, Edith, if I only thought . . .

Edith Hush, Henry. Tonight, let us be . . . husband and wife.

Henry How glad it makes me to hear those words. I know you find me cold, Edith.

Edith Your business absorbs your time and . . . energy.

Henry Distant, you said. Cold and distant.

Edith Let tonight be our second honeymoon. I propose to leave tomorrow.

Henry So soon?

Edith Yes. Before I change my mind. All we need are our travelling bags and two tickets. I'll plan as I go along.

Henry Good gracious, how ridiculously young I feel! I do believe we'll have champagne with our dinner tonight.

Edith (*smiling*) Let it be the finest vintage. And we'll toast Mr Hardy.

Henry Yes, let's do that.

Edith The architect of my fortunes.

Henry Of ours.

Edith Of ours. We'll have the champagne chilled . . . yes . . . and the double-bed aired.

He kisses her, rather clumsily. She allows him to hold it for a few seconds, then pulls away, her face radiant with a smile not meant for her husband

CURTAIN

ACT II

SCENE 1

The same. An afternoon in October

Henry and Arnold are discovered, with drinks

Henry Will you propose a toast, Arnold?
Arnold To a new era.
Henry A new era.

They touch their glasses and drink

Arnold An era of prosperity. To Allied Wessex Wines.
Henry Allied Wessex Wines.

They drink

I could have insisted on Harnham and Slocombe, you know.
Arnold Ah, but we were not talking of winners and losers, were we? Allied
Wessex Wines is better. It might stand for All-Western Winners.
Henry (*savouring the phrase*) All-Western Winners. How apt. Five months
is a long time in the wine trade. Or should I say business?
Arnold And you have had the better of them. (*Expansively*) Yes, I admit it.
Though how you improved your turnover to such an extent I have no
idea.
Henry I sharpened my knife, Arnold. But let's have no more of that.
There's no need for knives now. As the senior partner, I propose they be
locked away.
Arnold (*moving to the window*) With all my heart. (*He looks out*) I see you
have the travelling fair here.
Henry It opens this evening. And what an infernal racket it will be making.
Quite ruins the peace of the neighbourhood.
Arnold Fairs make a cheery sound. I used to love them in my youth.
Henry You know, Arnold, you and I have got to know each other better
over the past few months. Our temperaments are far apart, but in one way
I envy you.
Arnold In what way?
Henry You *still* have the youthful spirit. I could almost imagine you
jumping on that hobby-horse and whirling around like a schoolboy.
Arnold I take that as a compliment.
Henry (*struck by a thought*) The hobby-horse, yes. I have a feeling the
business is something of a hobby with you.

Arnold Well, it's certainly not a matter of life and death. I have some capital set aside. Failure would not have meant the end of the world.

Henry That's the difference between us. Business is my reason for living. For me, failure *would* have meant the end.

Arnold (*startled*) You don't mean ... literally?

Henry (*nodding*) Literally.

Arnold (*uneasy*) Oh, come, isn't your lovely wife reason enough for living?

Henry Ah, my wife. That reminds me. She's coming home next week.

Arnold With that girl—what was her name?

Henry Anna. You must come over to dinner.

Arnold By all means.

Henry But I must not keep you. I know you have an appointment. (*He rings the bell*) I shall telephone you directly she arrives. Things are going well. Even the telephone is improving by leaps and bounds.

Betty enters

Betty Yes, sir?

Henry Get Mr Slocombe's hat and coat and see him out. Then come back here.

Betty Yes, sir.

She goes out with Arnold

Henry preens himself self-importantly, humming tunelessly, adjusting his tie etc.

Betty returns

Henry Ah, Betty, I want to talk to you.

Betty To me, sir? I ain't done anything wrong, sir, have I?

Henry You have been looking very flustered of late. You must try to control it.

Betty Well, sir, with all the excitement ...

Henry Excitement is no excuse for whirling around like a top. Mr Hardy will be here shortly. When he comes, I want you to show him in with decorum.

Betty (*blankly*) Sir?

Henry With *dignity*, Betty. The world will go on at the same pace, so you might as well do so too.

Betty Oh, lor, sir, I dunno whether I'm coming or going, and that's a fact.

Henry You mean the business over at the Assizes?

Betty That, sir, and the mistress coming home next week, and Anna and all.

Henry Let's take one thing at a time, shall we? I'm as keen as you are to know what's going on at the Assizes. But we must await the arrival of the *Late Extra* on the stand outside. Directly it's here, I want you to go out and buy a copy and bring it to me. Slowly. With dignity. At least wait for the ink to dry.

Betty Yes, sir. Do you think ... ?

Henry What I think is academic.

The doorbell rings

Ah, that will be Mr Hardy. Proceed at an easy pace, admit him, take his hat and coat and show him in here. Is that clear?

Betty Right away, sir. (*She starts to hurry out*)

Henry Easy, Betty, *easy*.

She walks out with self-conscious slowness

Henry resumes his tie-adjusting routine, then places himself at the window, where he stands looking out

Hardy enters, sweeping in ahead of Betty

Hardy It's all right, Betty, no need to announce me. Off you go.

Henry Oh, Betty.

Betty Yes, sir?

Henry Don't forget the *Late Extra*. The moment it's on the stand.

Betty I shan't forget, sir.

Betty exits, even more slowly than the last time

Henry I'm glad to see you, Mr Hardy.

Hardy Well, what is your news?

Henry So much, I scarcely know where to begin. (*He waves Hardy to the settee*)

Hardy (*sitting*) No hurry, no hurry. I see you were observing the fair.

Henry Yes. Tonight it all starts again.

Hardy I like these travelling fairs. All that marvellous iron machinery. The laughter, the gaiety. But I'm too old for its pleasures, I fear.

Henry It takes me back to last year. When it all began.

Hardy When Anna first met Mr Raye.

Henry Yes, indeed. And now Anna is on her way back from Italy.

Hardy She is?

Henry And Mr Raye is at the Assizes, making Lord knows what sensation, and——

Hardy (*holding up his hand*) Wait, wait. I have only just arrived. You are ahead of me, Mr Harnham.

Henry The fair. I may say, without putting it too highly, that the advent of the fair last year was the foundation of my present good fortune.

Hardy Your present good fortune?

Henry Anna met Mr Raye. And a secondary consequence was that you came to me. By recommendation of that same Mr Raye. And you were good enough to recommend me in turn to many of your friends in Dorchester.

Hardy What of it? You know your business. I was glad to be of help.

Henry Oh, yes, I know my business. But it was slipping through my fingers. It was going to Arnold Slocombe.

Hardy I understood that Slocombe dealt with the cheaper end.

Henry To a point, yes. But his expansion in that line was allowing him to make incursions into mine.

Hardy Well?

Henry Well, sir, thanks to you, I was able to reverse the trend.

Hardy I'm glad to hear it.

Henry To the point where there was no longer room for both his business and mine.

Hardy And so?

Henry Slocombe was here, in this very room, a few minutes ago. There is now only one wine business, where before there were two. (*With pompous pride*) You are addressing the senior partner of Allied Wessex Wines.

Hardy I see. A merger?

Henry Between ourselves, more like an acquisition. No matter how the details are dressed up.

Hardy (*with a delicate irony lost on Henry*) Congratulations.

Henry Oh, yes, the firm of Slocombe is now part of the Harnham business. I was about to say "empire", but we must not get too grandiose.

Hardy (*as before*) Of course not.

Henry We are now, if I may include my friend Arnold, the most important wine merchants in Wiltshire and Dorset.

Hardy How very gratifying. But you flatter me too much by ascribing it to my own humble efforts.

Henry You think so? Well, of course it would have come sooner or later in any case. But credit where it's due. You speeded the process. You started the word. And the word got around. When it was seen that people like your influential friends—your *titled* friends—were placing large orders with me, the rest were quick to follow.

Hardy I'm glad to know it. I have not heard a single complaint.

Henry (*sententiously*) It is not only the wheels that make a business turn over, but the wheels within wheels.

Hardy And the rest of your news?

Henry Everything seems to be happening all at once. I had a letter from my wife this morning. She will be home next week with Anna.

Hardy Splendid tidings.

Henry She hints at good news of her own.

Hardy About Anna, I expect. Perhaps she has succeeded in chipping away at her rougher edges. Your wife is an excellent woman. I am sure she would make a fine tutor.

Henry (*dismissively*) Oh, she'll never make much of that one. Anna is a pretty little peasant, and that's that. Yet she married our fine young barrister, and we all have to make the best of it.

Hardy I was under the impression it was the young barrister who was doing that.

Henry At present he has other fish to fry. Did you know that he is, even now, distinguishing himself at the Assizes?

Hardy In what capacity?

Henry He is engaged as junior counsel for the defence of Minnie Castle.

Hardy Is he, by God? The unfortunate woman charged with the murder of her child?

Henry (*with satisfaction*) I *thought* that would surprise you.

Hardy A hopeless case, as I understand.

Henry Even more hopeless now, according to some who should know.

Betty charges in, out of breath and clutching a newspaper

Betty It's come, sir. *Late Extra.*

Henry (*taking the paper*) Thank you.

Betty is lingering

That will be all, Betty.

Betty Yes, sir.

She exits, reluctantly

Hardy Well?

Henry Counsel for the defence was appointed by the court. The defendant is poor, and required legal aid. The man chosen was Lawrence Braithwaite.

Hardy A competent gentleman, so I've heard.

Henry His competence at this moment is open to question. He was taken ill this morning. We have been waiting hourly to hear the outcome.

Hardy And Charles Raye was engaged as his junior, you say?

Henry (*scanning the paper*) Ah, here we are. (*Reading*) "Assizes Sensation." No, really! Is it possible?

Hardy Will you do me the goodness to read it aloud, sir?

Henry (*reading*) "The trial of Minnie Castle at the Assizes was dramatically interrupted this morning by the sudden illness of her counsel, Mr Lawrence Braithwaite. He was afflicted with stomach cramps when making his way to the court, where he was about to open the case for the defence."

Hardy A sensation indeed. Go on.

Henry (*reading*) "The case was suspended while the Judge, Mr Justice Latimer, conferred in chambers with crown counsel Mr Leonard Harvey, QC, and with junior defence council Mr Charles Raye. We have just heard that the said Mr Raye will personally take over the conduct of the case, following a medical bulletin to the effect that Mr Braithwaite is suffering from aggravated food poisoning, and will be indisposed for at least another week."

Hardy I wonder they didn't adjourn the case to a later date.

Henry Wait. (*He scans the paper*) It seems an adjournment was refused, owing to the heavy log of cases down for hearing.

Hardy (*impatiently*) Yes, yes, read on.

Henry (*reading*) "Mr Raye is understood to have assured the judge of the defendant's complete confidence in himself."

Hardy So she trusts our Mr Raye. How very fortunate for him!

Henry (*laying down the paper*) More likely she is without hope. The evidence against her is quite damning.

Hardy I remember the advance publicity. Miss Castle is a lady of easy virtue, is she not?

Henry (*shaking his head*) A bad case. She smothered her child. She was preparing to dispose of it in a box when she was apprehended.

Hardy At least she must be presumed innocent until found guilty.

Henry Oh, there is no doubt of her guilt. None at all. One of her neighbours testified, in terms, that the defendant had asked her: "How can you get rid of a child?" Those were her exact words. She did not deny them.

Hardy Ah, that I didn't know. Then things do look black.

Henry Well, at least it will be valuable experience for Mr Raye. It will bring his name into the public eye.

Hardy Yes, there is a certain gallantry about defending a hopeless case. Any publicity is good publicity, eh? So Braithwaite's illness is providential. Anna will be mightily proud of her husband, whatever the outcome.

Henry Will she? I wonder. Is she capable of knowing what it means for him to be leading for the defence in a murder trial?

Hardy She is capable of knowing he is making a noise in the world.

Henry What a pity he had to throw his life away on such a senseless clod. And all through the animal passions of a moment. Men are such weak vessels.

Hardy Without those animal passions, there would be no literature.

Henry And no great loss to the world, I daresay. No offence to you, for my wife tells me you dabble a bit yourself.

Hardy I am an incurable dabbler, Mr Harnham.

Henry Ah, if men could only restrain their baser natures, think what a happier world ours would be.

Hardy I should not care to live in such a world. You are a Christian, are you not?

Henry I hope I am.

Hardy Without sin, there would be no Christianity. The one gives rise to the other. Is not man's weakness the very basis of religion? Ours is an imperfect world, and I would not have it otherwise. The passions are the cosmic forces that mould mankind. Even Mr Raye depends on them, you see. He would not thank you for a Garden of Eden. Where would he make his living?

Henry (*anxious to change the subject*) Have you seen him lately?

Hardy Not for months.

Henry Now that his wife is returning, he and his sister are staying here as my guests.

Hardy (*with a recollective smile*) Ah, his sister . . .

Henry Between ourselves, she rules his life. He never moves but in her shadow.

Hardy She has a forceful personality.

Henry (*severely*) Self-absorbed is the word, sir. She has no interest in anything that does not impinge on her own affairs.

Hardy Or her brother's, surely?

Henry All motivation and no moral sense. When she wants something she goes for it, and devil take the hindmost.

Hardy She certainly guards her brother's interests with uncommon zeal.

The door flies open and Charlotte herself comes bustling in

Why, Miss Raye, we were just talking about you.

Charlotte (*waving a finger in mock reproof*) Naughty, naughty. And what brings you here, Mr Hardy?

Henry I asked him. I have just finalized the Slocombe deal.

Charlotte (*airily*) Oh, I know all about that.

Henry (*peeved*) You know?

Charlotte I've been talking to him. A merger, I believe?

Hardy (*with a smile*) More an acquisition, it seems.

Henry The fulfilment of a long-held ambition.

Charlotte Let's hope it turns out well for you.

Hardy (*smoothly warding off the note of acrimony that has crept into the conversation*) I hear your brother is about to make a name for himself, Miss Raye.

Charlotte (*on what is currently her favourite subject*) He can hardly do worse than Braithwaite. That man had practically thrown the case away. A born whiffler. No wonder he's got stomach cramps. Imagine, if that poor wretch had been a rich woman, she could have been defended by the finest QC in the land. That's British justice for you!

Henry (*deeply affronted*) Surely you would not criticize our legal system?

Charlotte Wouldn't I, though? What *is* justice, Mr Harnham?

Henry Finding out the truth, of course. Without fear or favour. (*Smugly*) And we British happen to do that better than anyone else in the world.

Charlotte So you say the truth will out, no matter who pleads her case?

Henry (*loftily*) That, Miss Raye, is why we have judges.

Charlotte Then what is to be gained by engaging one counsel above another, at vast expense?

Hardy She's got you there, sir.

Charlotte British justice has its price, like other commodities. Your wine, for instance. You get what you pay for. And if you have no money, you get—(*with deep scorn*)—Braithwaite.

Henry (*coldly*) I don't care to hear you speak so slightingly about our most hallowed institutions. Besides, the woman is plainly guilty.

Charlotte I hope you will stay and meet my brother, Mr Hardy.

Hardy Not for the world would I miss that pleasure.

Henry Good. (*But he is plainly out of countenance, and gives Charlotte a baleful glance*) And now, if you'll excuse me, I have much to see to.

He gives a formal bow and walks out, head high, much on his dignity

Charlotte (*breaking into a peal of laughter*) Oh, dear, he's priceless!

Hardy You offended him.

Charlotte He'll get over it.

Hardy A shrewd man of business. And a grateful one.

Charlotte Grateful?

Hardy He seems to hold me in some measure responsible for his good fortune. I was able to expand his business somewhat.

Charlotte And now he has Slocombe under his thumb. (*A pause*) Or thinks he has.

Hardy Only thinks?

Charlotte I've got my eye on Arnold Slocombe. He needs someone to look after his interests.

Hardy A wife?

Charlotte (*with a knowing smile*) Perhaps. Harnham can be handled. By the right person. He may be a shrewd businessman, but in some respects he is a fool. God's typical Englishman.

Hardy (*with playful irony*) A proper Christian gentleman.

Charlotte In a land teeming with them.

Hardy Would I suppose you are not enamoured of your country, Miss Raye?

Charlotte Let us say I am not enamoured of humbug.

Hardy Take care. You are his guest.

Charlotte Ah, Mr Hardy, if only I had your manners.

Hardy (*chuckling*) You would not know what to do with them.

Charlotte His wife is made of different clay. Now there's a woman I can admire. Why she married him is a mystery.

Hardy Not really. She felt she was getting past the springtime of life. And better a prosperous husband than a poor one.

Charlotte You talk like a cynic.

Hardy I speak of the world's values.

Charlotte To hell with the world's values!

Hardy They will not go there so easily. Certainly not in England.

Charlotte They are not fixed for all time. They will change.

Hardy And are changing. But the process is slow. I see a future time when the Minnie Castles of this world will not be hanged at all.

Charlotte (*stoutly*) A future time? Stuff and nonsense! Next week, you just see, Miss Castle will be acquitted!

Hardy I applaud your faith in your brother. Why, here he is!

Charles strides into the room, the picture of confidence, and warmly shakes Hardy's hand

Charles How good to see you, Mr Hardy. I didn't expect to find you here.

Hardy I was invited over to congratulate Mr Harnham. Now it seems I must congratulate you. I hear you are doing great things at the Assizes.

Charles Not yet. The feeling of the court is that the noose is round her neck already.

Charlotte You wouldn't believe the prejudice, Mr Hardy. You could cut it with a knife.

Charles Yet I have a trick or two up my sleeve.

Charlotte The press have poisoned the air against her. She has been found guilty ten times over.

Charles The poor woman appears to have accepted her fate.

Hardy That's hardly surprising, given the power of the press.

Charles They try her because she is a prostitute. They try her because her child was illegitimate. They try her because she cannot quote Scripture.

Hardy (*with a smile*) I suppose they also try her for the words on the indictment?

Charlotte But Charles will show them yet. Won't you, Charles?

Hardy You really believe she did not kill the child?

Charles I believe only in facts that can be proved.

Hardy That was not quite the question.

Charles Then, in the absence of good proof, I believe her innocent.

Hardy And your theory?

Charles That the child smothered itself accidentally in the cot. The mother left it sleeping with its head in the pillow. Motherhood is a craft not much studied by prostitutes.

Hardy Yet she hid the child away, did she not, and tried to conceal its death?

Charles That cannot be disputed. She was a frightened woman. But does that make her a murderess?

Hardy I understand she practically confessed.

Charlotte (*grimly*) The police don't wear kid gloves when interrogating people like her.

Charles And that means I'm going to be a very busy man. Thank goodness the charming wanderer is not coming home till next week.

Hardy The prospect of her return does not distract you?

Charles On the contrary, it inspires me. (*With enthusiasm*) So long since she went away. Were it not for the case, I could hardly wait.

Hardy I expect you will find her much changed.

Charles Oh, I don't think so. Still the same delightful, cultivated lady.

Hardy I do beg your pardon. I thought we were talking about your wife.

Charles Oh, yes, my wife. Her as well. Of course it will give me great pleasure to see her.

Hardy And it will give your host great pleasure to see the other. I think that is a just division.

Charles (*with restrained bitterness*) Oh, we are speaking of justice, are we?

Hardy (*pointedly*) It has its price. As your sister was saying just now.

Charlotte I was referring to British justice. There is a higher one.

Hardy How did your leader come to be struck down so suddenly, Mr Raye? I can think of no parallel in British jurisprudence.

Charlotte The internal economy obeys its own laws, even in Britain. He seems to have gone down with food poisoning.

Hardy No idea how it happened?

Charles None at all. Charlotte and I took breakfast with him at his hotel. He was as right as rain then. We were discussing the case.

Hardy And how did he rate your client's chances?

Charles Not highly.

Charlotte Let's call a spade a spade. He rated them as nil. He is a dunce. He kept on bleating that it was only a show trial.

Hardy (*thoughtfully*) Then his illness seems to have been ...

Charlotte Been what, Mr Hardy?

Hardy Bless my soul, I was almost going to say *fortunate*.

Charles It was certainly so for me. Does that sound terrible?

Hardy One often finds that one man's misfortune is another's opportunity. That is the balance of nature.

Charles (*dispelling the uneasy atmosphere with a light quip*) Well, I need to restore nature's balance by taking a bath. I decline to work on the case till I've had my dinner. Tomorrow's Saturday. Two vital witnesses to interview, one client to consult and a lengthy brief to work on. The time will fly till the travellers come home.

He bows to Hardy and exits

Charlotte As for me, I'm off to have a look at the fair. It opens this evening. (*Preparing to go*) It will give me an appetite for dinner. There must be some enchantment about that fair, Mr Hardy. I want to know what madness seized Charles on that day.

Hardy You care for your brother a great deal.

Charlotte He's the only one I've got. He needs someone of character to protect his interests.

Hardy An advocate's advocate?

Charlotte If you like. I suppose you would not care to accompany me?

Hardy I think not. I've stayed too long already. Enjoy yourself, Miss Raye.

Charlotte exits

He strolls over to the window

Hardy A very remarkable lady. (*He waves to her from the window*) Braithwaite's misfortune. Her brother's opportunity. There she goes. So self-possessed.

Betty enters, carrying a book

Betty Oh, sir, I'm looking for Miss Raye. Has she gone?

Hardy She left just now to have a look at the fair. Is it important?

Betty It's this book, sir. I found it in her room when I was tidying up. I think it belongs to the master, but I can't be sure.

Hardy Let me see it. (*He takes it from her, then draws in his breath in surprise*) Erskine's *Toxicology*!

Betty What's that, sir?

Hardy Only a medical volume, Betty. Wait. (*He sits at the desk and scribbles a note*) "This book returned—with the compliments of—Thomas Hardy". (*He puts the note between the leaves of the book, like a bookmark, with the top sticking out*) Betty, I want you to return this book to Miss Raye's room.

Betty To Miss Raye's room. Yes, sir.

Hardy Leave this note exactly where it is. Is that clear?

Betty (*taking the book*) Yes, sir.

Hardy And now I must be about my business. Tell your master I'll be back next week. For the verdict.

Betty For the verdict, sir. Got it.

Hardy And the end of the story.

Betty What story, sir?

Hardy Just say the end of the story. The last piece of the jigsaw puzzle. No
need to see me out, Betty.

He exits

Betty stands for a moment, looking puzzled

Betty The last piece of the jigsaw puzzle. Sounds a bit daft to me. (*She
giggles*) Oh, well, that's life.

She goes out, clutching the book

CURTAIN

SCENE 2

The same. A Thursday evening, six days later

The window is open. Fairground music and voices are heard from outside

Edith and Anna enter, followed by Betty

Anna Well, here we are again, then.
Edith Yes. Back at last.
Betty A year to the day since——
Anna Since what, Betty?
Betty Since you was at the fair.
Anna Since you *were* at the fair.

*It will be clear that Anna's accent has acquired a touch of polish, though she
speaks in a slightly stilted and unnatural tone of voice. Edith favours her with a
stern look for having corrected Betty*

Edith Close the window and draw the curtains, will you, Betty?
Betty Yes, madam. (*She closes the window and draws the curtains*)

The music ceases

  I was just airing it a bit, like.
Edith Quite right. The weather's warm for autumn.
Anna Most clement.

Betty reacts to this remark with an amazed stare

Edith Where's the master, Betty?
Betty He wasn't expecting you till tomorrow, madam. He's over to the
Assizes.
Edith The Assizes? I've never known him go there.
Betty Oh, madam, it's awful exciting! There's a big murder trial. The
lawyer's ill, and Mr Charles Raye took his place.
Anna (*overcome, back to her own manner*) Charles! A murder trial! Cor!

Edith As you say, Anna, cor! we need bringing up-to-date, don't we?

Arnold enters

Betty (*baulked of her story*) Here's Mr Slocombe. I 'spect he'll tell you all about it.

Edith Good-evening, Mr Slocombe. (*To Betty*) Off you go now, Betty. We'll have a talk later.

Betty Yes, madam.

Betty exits

Edith Mr Slocombe, this is my travelling companion, Mrs Charles Raye.

Arnold How do you do, Mrs Raye.

Anna Very well, thank you, Mr Slocombe.

Edith It seems much has been afoot since we went away. Tell me about the Assizes, Mr Slocombe.

Arnold Your husband has kept me fully informed about your trip, Mrs Harnham. Did you know we are partners now?

Edith No, really? I'm delighted. He hinted in his letters that there was something in the wind.

Anna (*speaking with care now, like a well-bred lady*) What do I hear about my husband taking over from a lawyer?

Arnold He is leading for the defence in the case of Regina versus Minnie Castle.

Anna Who's Minnie Castle?

Arnold A murderess. I beg your pardon, a presumed murderess. The verdict is expected today. That's why Mr Harnham is in court. He's with Charlotte Raye.

Edith And how is Charlotte?

Arnold As busy as ever. She has been good enough to advise me on the running of my affairs.

Anna (*darkly*) She's an old busybody, if you ask me. Sister-in-law or no sister-in-law.

Edith Now, Anna, let's not be uncharitable. (*To Arnold*) Tell me about the lawyer's illness, Mr Slocombe.

Arnold It was food poisoning. Miss Raye's the one to ask about that. She talks most learnedly about the symptoms.

Anna Defending a murderess, eh?

Edith A *presumed* murderess, Anna.

Anna Same difference.

Edith Same *thing*, you mean. Which, of course, it isn't. It's not the same thing at all.

Arnold I believe you ladies have lately been in Italy.

Edith Yes.

Arnold And how did you find it?

Anna We took the train.

Edith No, no, Anna, he meant how *was* it?

Anna Oh, I see. Hot and uncomfortable.

Edith Anything else?

Anna (*parrot-fashion*) Italy is a land of marked contrast and great natural beauty. But political stability is lacking.

Arnold Really?

Edith I'm sure Mr Slocombe doesn't want to hear about that, Anna.

Arnold No, go on, I'm fascinated.

Anna (*as before*) Newly unified some thirty years ago from a collection of states under foreign domination, Italy is still in search of a true national identity.

Arnold (*bemused*) Fancy that.

Anna (*back to her own manner, having exhausted her knowledge on the subject*) Apart from that, it was hot and uncomfortable.

Arnold Well, if you'll excuse me, I must go and see if the latest edition is on the stand yet. I'll see you later.

He exits

Edith There, now, Anna, you've driven him away.

Anna (*bridling*) *I* have? I like that!

Edith Don't take on. You have made wonderful progress. But you must not spoil it by flaunting your newly acquired knowledge.

Anna (*sulkily*) What's knowledge for if not to be used?

Edith You may introduce it into conversation, but only in its natural context.

Anna What's context?

Edith If the subject comes up, and you feel you can make a useful contribution.

Anna (*still sulky*) He asked me how Italy was, didn't he?

Edith Yes. And you told him hot and uncomfortable. Not perhaps the most original of observations, but adequate. The political stability was quite extraneous.

Anna What's extraneous?

Edith I bring in these words only to show that you still have a lot to learn. You must take things at their natural pace, not try to run before you can walk. Extraneous is surplus to requirements.

Anna I see.

Edith Education is not just learning a few facts. I want you to be a credit to your husband, as he is a credit to you.

Anna (*still smarting*) You corrected me in front of Mr Slocombe.

Edith I would not have done so, Anna, but for one thing. You did the same to Betty. When she said "since you was at the fair".

Anna I wasn't trying to show her up, honest.

Edith Then let it be a lesson. Never try to impress those less fortunate than yourself. It might rebound on you.

Voices off

Anna Oh, listen, I can hear them coming!

Charles, Charlotte and Henry enter

Charles Well! So the wanderers have returned!

Henry We heard you were back.

He goes to Edith, who submits to a formal embrace

How are you, Edith? I was not expecting you till tomorrow.

Anna (*rushing to her husband*) Charles, darling!

Charlotte Well, Charles, aren't you going to embrace your wife?

Charles (*doing so, but with a notable lack of ardour*) Anna, my dear, how well you are looking.

Anna Have you missed me?

Charles (*with a glance at Edith*) I've been counting the days.

Henry I trust you are both well.

Edith Yes, Henry. I have much news to tell you. And you have some for me. I saw Mr Slocombe just now.

Henry Then he's beaten me to it.

Edith Not really. He left it to you to give me the details.

Charlotte And Charles has news for you too, Anna.

Charles But first, I want to hear about your voyaging.

Anna I'm a different woman now, Charles. I'm going to be a great credit to you, just you see.

Charles How refined your speech is. Isn't it, Charlotte?

Charlotte Italy seems to have had a beneficial effect. Italy . . . or Edith.

Anna (*breathlessly*) We went to Florence—or Firenze, as we call it—and visited the Uffizi Gallery. And Rome, where we saw the Vatican and the Swiss Guard and the Sistine Chapel and——

Edith (*laughing*) Not so fast, Anna! You'll exhaust our itinerary in five minutes.

Anna Oh, and Milan, to La Scala.

Charles You went to the opera?

Edith We saw *The Sicilian Vespers*.

Anna (*pronouncing correctly but stiltedly*) *I Vespri Siciliani.* It's by Giuseppe Verdi, you know.

Charlotte (*sotto voce*) My God, I don't believe it!

Anna (*hearing and misunderstanding*) Oh, yes, Charlotte, I assure you. Verdi, the greatest of all Italian composers and patriots.

Charles Patriots?

Edith (*warningly*) Anna!

Anna No, he asked—didn't you, darling?

Charles Er—oh, yes, I asked.

Henry (*his patience fraying*) I'm sure this is all very interesting, but Charles is simply bursting with his own news.

Anna (*getting well into her stride*) Verdi was a great hero of the Risorgimento. (*Again she pronounces the word correctly, but has to pick her way carefully through the syllables: ree-zorr-jee-men-to*)

Henry Risorgi . . . ?

Anna The unifaction of Italy.

Edith Unification, dear.

Anna Unification. They made him a senator. Did you know that they used the letters of his name as a secret sign? I bet you didn't. V.E.R.D.I. It

meant Vittorio Emmanuele Re D'Italia. That's Victor Emmanuel King of
   Italy.
Charlotte Fascinating. Unbelievable.
Edith Anna, Anna!
Henry Chatter, chatter.
Charles (*to Anna*) You've picked up a great deal of useful knowledge, I see.
Anna Oh, that's not all.
Charles It's enough for now. Don't you want to hear my news?
Anna 'Course I do, darling.
Charlotte The trial. Did Mr Slocombe tell you about the trial?
Edith Yes. *And* about the lawyer's illness.
Charlotte He's almost recovered now, you'll be glad to hear.
Henry But you haven't heard the best of it yet. Go on, Charles, tell them
   what happened.
Charles Minnie Castle has just walked from the court a free woman.
Charlotte Not Guilty. And quite right too.
Henry I was wrong. I admit it. The case looked as black as could be. And
   Charles got her off with his advocacy.
Charles Correction. I got her off because she was innocent.
Charlotte (*pointedly, looking at Henry*) Of course the truth will out, no
   matter who pleads the case.
Charles It was a damned close-run thing, though.
Charlotte The biggest stumbling block was what the accused had said to a
   neighbour: "How can you get rid of a baby?"
Edith But that sounds like a confession.
Charlotte So the jury thought. Until Charles made the neighbour admit
   that she might have said: "How *can* you get rid of a baby?" You see?
   Different emphasis, different meaning. How can *anyone*, least of all a
   loving mother, *possibly* get rid of a *baby*?
Edith Astonishing.
Henry I'd never have thought of it in a million years.
Charlotte And then the medical evidence. Children do smother themselves
   accidentally in their cots. Charles dug out several attested cases. And
   Minnie got the benefit of the doubt.
Anna Fancy getting a murderess off! I'm proud of you, Charles.
Charles Good heavens, proud of me for getting a murderess off! I restored
   an innocent woman to freedom.
Charlotte (*severely*) Yes, Anna, remember that.
Henry Even if she was a prostitute.
Anna Oh, she was, was she? (*As if it implied guilt*) Well, then.
Charles What do you mean, "well, then"? Her calling had nothing to do
   with it.
Anna She was up to no good, if you ask me.
Charlotte No-one did.
Henry (*pompously*) We must concede the girl a point. The jury are entitled
   to take background into account.
Charlotte I see. You mean they should award points for morality?
Henry I meant that a married lady, for example, with a child born in

honour, may be presumed to act from higher motives than a girl of the
streets with a child of shame.

Charles I am a lawyer. Fact and act: those are the only things that concern
me. I clear my mind of all else.

Edith Child of shame. That sounds rather lurid to me.

Henry You know very well what I meant, my dear.

Edith Are there not *degrees* of shame?

Henry (*as if talking to a child*) It's very simple. A child not born of the
woman's lawful husband.

Edith Can one always be sure?

Henry This woman didn't have a husband. Only clients.

Edith Yes, Henry. Now tell me about your agreement with Arnold Slocombe.

Henry Oh, Slocombe. I've taken him over.

Charlotte The big fish swallowing the smaller fish, eh?

Henry (*coldly*) Your marine parallels are very interesting, Miss Raye. We
are now Allied Wessex Wines. Arnold will thank me in due time.

Charlotte For being eaten?

Henry For being rescued. There comes a time when two rival concerns have
to come together, or the lesser will perish. It's a law of nature.

Charlotte Well, it seems to be a law of *commerce*.

Henry (*waxing lyrical*) I see the day coming when all business everywhere
will be in the hands of a few giants. Spreading across national frontiers.
Encompassing the globe. Improved production! Greater efficiency! Prosperity for all!

Charlotte In short, a general paradise?

Henry Why not?

Charlotte Controlled by Henry Harnham, no doubt.

Anna Well, I find it all very boring.

Hardy enters

Hardy (*having caught the last remark*) What is boring?

Henry Ah, Mr Hardy. I was beginning to think you would not be in time
for dinner.

Edith (*warmly*) How good to see you again, Mr Hardy.

Hardy You are looking well. And you, Mrs Raye.

Anna Thanks.

Charlotte We were talking about commerce. Mr Harnham was putting the
case for the rise of giants. A brave new world.

Hardy Well, we certainly have a giant here today. Mr Raye, you will make a
great name for yourself. Your advocacy was masterly.

Charlotte That's praise indeed, from such an authority.

Hardy I never saw the tables turned in a court so quickly.

Charlotte Good advocates are rare these days.

Hardy Yes. Speaking of which, I understand the patient is much improved.

Charlotte Patient? Oh, you mean the lawyer Braithwaite? It was only a
passing illness.

Hardy Yes. (*A pause*) I wonder what would have become of Minnie Castle
   if it had not happened.
Henry It's no good speculating. It *did* happen.
Hardy We writers live by speculation.
Edith I see we are back to your jigsaw puzzle again.
Charlotte I must thank you for returning that book, Mr Hardy.
Hardy It was nothing.
Charlotte I had no idea I'd left it lying around.
Charles What book was that?
Charlotte (*for once nonplussed*) Why, it was, er . . .
Hardy A novel, Mr Raye.
Charlotte Yes, that's right, a novel.
Hardy A mystery, if I recall.
Charlotte The mystery is how it came into your hands.
Hardy (*turning to Anna*) Mrs Raye, are you interested in theatre?
Edith I took her to the opera in Milan.
Hardy I meant theatre without singing.
Anna Why?
Hardy The Assizes today became the purest form of theatre. And your
   husband was the leading actor.
Anna (*blankly*) Fancy.
Hardy As the wife of a great actor, you are going to be much in the public
   eye.
Anna I don't understand.
Charles I'm only a lawyer.
Hardy You do yourself an injustice. Lawyers are two a penny. The greatest
   advocates often know little law. They leave that to their clerks. No, sir,
   you are an actor.
Charlotte *I* know what you mean. (*Her tone plainly suggests that no-one else
   does*) Go on.
Hardy An English murder trial. Was there ever such pure theatre? Two
   gladiators ranged in combat, and some poor wretch's neck at stake. Who
   needs lawyers? A lawyer may cite precedent all day. It takes an *actor* to
   change the meaning of a vital sentence by rearranging the emphasis of a
   single word.
Henry Well, well, we live and learn.
Hardy Mr Braithwaite knows a deal of law. But would he have spotted the
   significance of getting rid of a baby?
Charlotte *He* would not know the significance of getting rid of a common
   cold.
Hardy (*pointedly*) Or contracting food poisoning?
Henry (*looking at his watch*) Soon be time for dinner. I've asked Slocombe.
   We'll be a party of seven.
Anna I could eat a horse.
Henry Edith, you hinted in your last letter that you had some good news.
Edith With all the excitement, I'd almost forgotten. It can wait till after
   dinner.
Henry As you wish. The suspense is whetting my appetite. Shall we go in?

Charles Let us go too, Anna.
Anna Yes, Charles.

Edith goes out with Henry, followed by Anna with Charles, leaving Hardy alone with Charlotte

Hardy Well, Miss Raye?
Charlotte Well, Mr Hardy?
Hardy You are an amazing woman.
Charlotte I would not say so.
Hardy I wonder if there is anything you could not do if you put your mind to it.
Charlotte I only put my mind to things I *can* do.
Hardy If you ever think about changing your station, you will make someone a very interesting wife.
Charlotte I'm working on it.
Hardy You should have time on your hands. Now that you have fairly launched your brother on his career.
Charlotte *I* have?
Hardy How is Mr Braithwaite?
Charlotte I would say he is in good health but low spirits.
Hardy You don't surprise me.
Charlotte On which count?
Hardy Both. *I* would say his good health has been nicely judged. And who would not be in low spirits, with his thunder stolen?
Charlotte He has no thunder to steal.
Hardy You've done some nursing in your time, I believe?
Charlotte Long ago, yes.
Hardy But you keep up-to-date?
Charlotte Don't we all?
Hardy Erskine's *Toxicology* is quite the standard reference book these days, isn't it?
Charlotte It is generally consulted.
Hardy I thought so.
Charlotte How careless of me to leave it lying around. (*A pause*) *Did* I leave it lying around, Mr Hardy?
Hardy We all make mistakes.
Charlotte Do we?
Hardy They have placed me at your right hand at dinner. Perhaps we can continue this discussion there. Until then, Miss Raye.

Hardy exits

Charlotte goes to the window and partly draws the curtains back. Fairground music is heard as she opens the window a few inches

Charlotte Oh, Charles, what a foolish boy you were at the fair.

Arnold enters

Arnold Good-evening, Miss Raye.

Charlotte Good-evening, Mr Slocombe. (*She shuts the window and draws the curtains across*)

The music ceases

Arnold I hope I'm not late for dinner.

Charlotte You are just in time, as usual.

Arnold How proud you must be of your brother.

Charlotte Charles is a clever man. And now he doesn't need me any more.

Arnold He needs *someone*.

Charlotte What do you mean?

Arnold To bring that wife of his up to the mark.

Charlotte (*with an amused smile*) Oh, *her*!

Arnold She's like a half-finished sculpture.

Charlotte A Galatea. But I fancy her Pygmalion has other matters in hand.

Arnold Indeed?

Charlotte Mrs Harnham's not going to have much time for our Anna from now on.

Arnold What makes you say that?

Charlotte I have eyes, Mr Slocombe. And ears.

Arnold Well, he's going to need a good wife.

Charlotte He's not alone in that.

Arnold A few months on the Continent, and she thinks she knows it all.

Charlotte She will learn. It's you I'm worried about just now.

Arnold And why should you be worried about me?

Charlotte You are going into partnership with Mr Harnham.

Arnold Well?

Charlotte If I know Mr Harnham, he intends to eat you up.

Arnold He may find me rather indigestible.

Charlotte Remember you are the junior partner.

Arnold His is the senior business.

Charlotte In point of years, yes.

Arnold And right now the more successful.

Charlotte Mr Harnham is a traditional trader. The question is: will he move with the times? New and dynamic ideas: that's what he needs.

Arnold That's where I intend to come in.

Charlotte If he lets you. You need someone to advise you.

Arnold I say, Miss Raye, isn't that going too far?

Charlotte I mean to make sure you go far *enough*.

Arnold (*nervously*) You? Where do you come into it?

Charlotte (*briskly*) Since my brother married Anna, my fortunes have somehow become intertwined with what one might call the Harnham problem. Anna was Edith Harnham's maid. Edith wrote her letters for her. Anna married my brother, but as Edith's substitute.

Arnold Substitute?

Charlotte That's what I said. And then Charles became Edith's lover in fact.

Arnold (*incredulously*) Do you know what you are saying, Miss Raye?

Charlotte Yes, Arnold. And you might as well call me Charlotte.

Arnold But this is slander, Miss, er, Charlotte.

Charlotte (*coolly*) I don't know about that. It happens to be true. And now you are to be Henry Harnham's partner. You are part of the Harnham problem, Arnold, whether you like it or not.

Arnold Well, I never!

Charlotte Part of *my* problem. That's why I told you. In confidence.

Arnold But I can't be bound by a confidence I haven't agreed to!

Charlotte Then you may consider yourself bound from this moment. You need a wife, Arnold.

Arnold A—a—a—wife?

Charlotte Stop dithering, Arnold. That's what I said.

Arnold But—but I'm a respectable widower.

Charlotte No widower is respectable.

Arnold Thank you for telling me.

Charlotte Not at all. I see in you a certain levity. You don't take anything seriously enough. Admit it: your business is only a hobby with you, isn't it?

Arnold You know, that's exactly what Harnham himself said.

Charlotte Which only goes to show that a man can't be wrong all the time. That's why he means to eat you. But I don't intend to let him, Arnold.

Arnold I'm much obliged for your concern, I'm sure.

Charlotte It will always be available. Your worries are over. And now let's go in to dinner, shall we?

Arnold (*with feeling*) I think we'd *better*.

Charlotte They have placed you at my left hand. I shall need you to counterbalance Mr Hardy, who will be at my right. He has a tiresome habit of talking about toxicology. That kind of thing is apt to spoil one's appetite. Come, Arnold.

Arnold (*meekly*) Yes, Charlotte.

He takes her arm and they go out as——

—the CURTAIN *falls*

SCENE 3

The same. Later the same evening

Charles and Anna enter

Anna I thought we'd never be alone.

Charles Well, we are now.

Anna (*embracing him impulsively*) Oh, darling, you don't know how I've waited for this moment.

Charles (*detaching himself, with tact and not unkindly*) You must restrain yourself, Anna. Someone might come in.

Anna I don't care if the Coldstream Guards come in. Dear Charles, I haven't seen you for months.

Charles Then we can wait a little longer. We have more than months ahead of us.

Anna (*sitting down, a little dejected*) If you say so.

Charles Did you enjoy your homecoming dinner?

Anna Oh, yes.

Charles It was quite a makeshift affair. You weren't expected until tomorrow. But you managed very well, my dear. This time you didn't complain the wine was sour.

Anna Oh, I'm used to wine now. We drank it all the time in Italy.

Charles Did you notice how well my sister and Arnold Slocombe were getting on together?

Anna Can't say I did. I only had eyes for you.

Charles She scarcely let Mr Hardy get a word in. I don't think you'd make much of a gossip, Anna. You are not very observant.

Anna Don't be so horrid, Charles.

Charles Well, tell me what you saw in the Uffizi Gallery.

Anna Pictures.

Charles Describe some of them.

Anna There was so many I couldn't take them all in.

Charles And the Sistine Chapel?

Anna (*brightly*) Oh, yes, the ceiling was all painted.

Charles (*sighing*) You make Michelangelo sound like a house painter. But never mind, I'm sure the tour has done you good. How was Mrs Harnham? Did she look after you well?

Anna She's the dearest, kindest creature in the world.

Charles Your loyalty does you credit, Anna. She has helped you a lot.

Anna Oh, yes, I know.

Charles I still have all those letters of hers. Written in your name.

Anna (*in a whining tone*) Charles, please don't bring all that up again.

Charles You need to be reminded now and then.

Anna I've been working ever so hard on my writing. She says I'm coming along famously.

Charles If you can form the characters and join them, I suppose that's something.

Anna What else is there?

Charles (*touching her on the forehead*) Mind, Anna. And spirit. Knowing exactly what to say. The right words.

Anna I would have written to you from Italy. I wanted to. But she said it'd be better if she sent you all our news herself.

Charles For which no doubt you were duly grateful.

Anna Dunno about that.

Charles She wrote in her own name this time. The same handwriting as those dear letters of—I was going to say yours.

Anna They *were* mine really. You know that.

Charles Do I?

Anna I *made* her write from Italy. Every day, nearly. I kept her at it.

Charles You don't need to worry about the pictures in the Uffizi. She sent me a full account of them all. The different impressions they made on her.

Anna *And on me.*

Charles Where you visited. The people you met. The gondoliers in Venice. The Roman postcard-sellers.

Anna I used to stand over her, making suggestions. But I never could make out her writing. Her loops and squiggles are kind of funny.

Charles She always mentioned you.

Anna I should hope she did! I always sent my love. But, darling, there's one thing I bet she never told you.

Charles And what's that?

Anna She's going to have a baby.

Charles What!

Anna (*utterly misreading the sensation she has created*) She's only thirty, you know.

Charles Good God!

Anna (*quietly pleased*) I know all about it. Would you like to hear?

Charles (*controlling his impatience*) I see you would like to tell me.

Anna She let her husband come to her room. The night before we left. She told me particular.

Charles Was it so unusual to let him come to her room?

Anna He hasn't been all he should. As a husband.

Charles You surprise me.

Anna You said I wasn't observant. But I knew, Charles, I knew. They were both in worlds of their own.

She notices his abstracted look

You aren't listening.

Charles (*quietly*) I hear you, Anna.

Anna But everything's fine between them now. It must be.

Charles To think that Mrs Harnham has got there before you.

Anna It wasn't my fault.

Charles I don't reproach you.

Anna 'Sides, there's no hurry. We've got our lives in front of us.

Charles A lot of living to get through.

Anna We've only been married seven months.

Charles (*drearily*) Seven whole months.

Anna And we'll have our own baby soon. Won't we?

Charles Perhaps. Provided you don't indulge your penchant for phantom pregnancies.

Anna What's a penchant?

Charles Taste. Liking.

Anna I said it wasn't my fault.

Charles Yet it was the decisive influence.

Anna What do you mean?

Charles In persuading me to marry you.

Anna But you *loved* me! (*A pause*) Didn't you?

Charles I loved your letters.

Anna (*twining her arms about him seductively*) You married me, Charles.
   That's all that matters. I've got you now.
Charles (*with a different emphasis*) Yes, Anna, you've got me.

Edith and Henry enter, in time to see them standing in apparent intimacy

Henry So this is where you two lovebirds have got to.
Charles (*giving an embarrassed cough as he breaks free*) Anna has been
   telling me all about your tour, Mrs Harnham.
Henry And your sister has got my new partner in a corner. They are getting
   on like the proverbial house on fire. Things have been going on under my
   very nose.
Edith How exciting.
Henry Don't you mean disturbing? Arnold is not a strong character. Now
   he's to be my partner, I feel responsible for him.
Charles You've roused my curiosity. Do you want a report?
Henry An opinion would do. You know your sister.
Charles Then we'll go and join them. Come, Anna.

Charles and Anna leave

Henry (*gloomily*) It's just as I thought.
Edith Charlotte and Arnold, you mean?
Henry I was speaking of Charles and Anna. Your efforts at education have
   not brought about much change. Or only on the surface. It was
   predictable.
Edith She really is learning.
Henry She speaks better, I grant you. But she has the soul of a servant.
Edith Of course, she's not very original.
Henry Her knowledge she repeats parrot-fashion. She doesn't understand a
   word.
Edith Give her time.
Henry With the right wife, that young man could go far. She will only drag
   him down.
Edith Perhaps you're right. (*Wearily*) I'll not argue.
Henry Of course I'm right. I wonder what induced him to marry her in the
   first place.
Edith The same might be said of many marriages. On one side or the other.
Henry But you still haven't given me your news. I daresay it's not very
   important, or you wouldn't have delayed it so long.
Edith It's for you to judge its importance, Henry.

She walks over to the window, leaving Henry DS, *with the maximum distance
separating them*

Henry Well, then, out with it!
Edith I'm going to have a baby.

The news takes a few seconds to sink in. He gazes at her open-mouthed

Henry A baby!
Edith A baby, Henry.

Henry (*moving towards her*) But this is *wonderful*!

He goes to embrace her, but the effect is clumsy and a little ludicrous, making her turn away

Edith You remember the night before I took Anna away?
Henry Of course. I spent the night in your room.
Edith Yes.
Henry Edith, I cannot understand you. Why did you not let me embrace you just now?
Edith There's no need for a demonstration.
Henry Good God, you don't even seem *pleased* at the news!
Edith It's not news to me. I have been living with it for quite a while.
Henry Look, Edith, it's time for plain speaking. Our married life has not been close. We have lived in separate rooms. But now—can't you see?— this makes a difference. To create another in our own image: this is the most precious gift a woman can bestow on a man.
Edith It's a biological imperative.
Henry Why must you use such arid terms to describe a *miracle*? I have long dreamed of such a thing—nurtured hopes—told myself that, in spite of everything, it would happen one day. And now, damn it, you're *indifferent*!

In a gesture of partial recognition, she puts her hands on his shoulders and gives him a chaste kiss

Edith Henry, I never knew you were so emotional.
Henry I am a man.
Edith Yes. But a man distant and preoccupied. A man wrapped up in his own business. A man to whom a wife is only another household chattel.
Henry (*turning away*) I'm sorry you thought that.
Edith What else could I think? And yet, within limits, I have tried to make you a good wife.
Henry Of course you have.
Edith I have run the house, engaged the servants, kept the accounts. We have never quarrelled in public.
Henry (*with empty longing*) Yet there's more to marriage than that.
Edith Marriage can be everything or nothing. Or as ours has been. Neither one thing nor the other. Existing in a twilight region.
Henry But I——
Edith No, please don't interrupt. You said it was time for plain speaking. I have been a wife and no wife. And now, by some extraordinary, unforeseen chain of events, I am to be a mother.
Henry Extraordinary? Unforeseen?
Edith Think how our lives have been changed by that servant girl.
Henry Anna? I haven't the slightest idea what you are talking about.
Edith The chain began when she met Charles Raye at the fair. A link was forged. They married. He sent Mr Hardy to you. Another link. As a result, your business flourished. You got what you would call the upper

hand over Arnold Slocombe. He is to be your partner. Aided and abetted, no doubt by Charles Raye's sister. How many links is that?

Henry You are being fanciful, Edith. All life is one event flowing from another. The important thing is that you are going to have a baby. Our baby. How does that link up with your chain?

Edith If I hadn't taken Anna away to be a better wife, would you have come to my room?

Henry I see your point.

Edith And now you must encourage the new couple. Charlotte needs a husband, as Arnold needs a wife.

Henry And what about me? I can deal with Arnold. But could I deal with Charlotte?

Edith (*smiling*) Could anyone deal with Charlotte? She is a law unto herself.

Henry A busy, meddling woman.

Edith A woman who knows her mind. A woman who could advance your business.

Henry Over my dead body! Business is man's work. As the home is woman's.

Edith Don't be too sure. The century is coming to an end. And with it a whole load of junk. Of stale ideas and borrowed thinking.

Henry (*pompously*) Those *stale ideas* have made our Empire great.

Edith (*shrugging*) Have it your own way.

Henry I intend to. Well, I'll go and keep an eye on them.

Edith Yes, Henry, you do that.

Henry Won't you come too?

Edith No, I'll join you later.

Charles enters

Henry Ah, there you are. What news?

Charles My sister is asking for you.

Henry Good. I was coming to see her anyway.

Henry exits

Charles Edith, I've been longing to speak to you. We haven't had a moment alone.

Edith Charles. Oh, my dear Charles!

She falls into his arms. They embrace for a few brief moments before she pulls away

We must be cautious.

Charles To hell with caution!

Edith No, Charles, no! We may be alone, but anyone could come in.

Charles Dear, prudent Edith.

Edith I hope you've been receiving my letters.

Charles I have them all. Every one. Bound in a neat bundle.

Edith Safe from inquisitive eyes, I hope?

Charles Absolutely. It was terrible, wanting to say so much to you but

knowing I could not reply. But wonderful also. To have letters signed in
your own name, not that wretched girl's.

Edith Charles, you are not to speak like that of your wife.

Charles You are my wife, Edith.

Edith It's madness to say so.

Charles Madness or not, it's true. Was it not madness on your part to send
me love letters?

Edith Yes. (*She smiles*) Anna stood at my shoulder sometimes, chattering
away like a tame bird. She *would* keep on telling me what to say.

Charles And you took no notice.

Edith No more than when I was writing in her name. It was like writing to
myself. Putting down my secret thoughts. Knowing that I should have no
answer.

Charles Here is my answer now. (*He kisses her*) I'm glad you poured out
your thoughts so freely. Yet there was one thing you chose not to tell me.

Edith What was that?

Charles Only the most important thing of all. Your *condition*, Edith.

Edith You know, then?

Charles Anna told me.

Edith I see. I was saving it till I saw you.

Charles I've been going mad since I heard. I must know. Is it mine?

Edith What do you think?

Charles I hardly dare guess. Anna told me your husband had visited your
room. The night before you left.

Edith Yes.

Charles So there must be a doubt.

Edith There is no doubt, dear Charles. I know my husband.

Charles How can you be so certain?

Edith Put your mind at rest. I know Henry's powers a good deal better than
he knows them himself. It was *necessary* to invite him to my room.

Charles (*recklessly*) Why? I would have been prepared to face the consequences.

Edith Of breaking *two* marriages?

Charles Of breaking two false ones, and putting one real one in their place.

Edith Then of causing two scandals. We would have been ruined, both of
us.

Charles Oh, Edith, you can be so calm, so *calculating*.

Edith Someone has to be.

Charles What did your husband say? You've told him, I suppose?

Edith He's delighted. I felt sorry for him. And ashamed. How can I deceive
him so?

Charles And what about us? Our whole life will be a deception.

Edith That's the price we must pay. I told Henry of the chain of events that
began with your visit to the fair last year. The links leading to the present.
Or those fit for him to hear. Of course he didn't begin to understand. But
for you, he would not now be taking Slocombe under his wing. Nor
would Charlotte.

Charles But for me, you would not now be an expectant mother.

Edith (*softly*) No. That's the secret link. Life seems a series of haphazard events. But every action brings its consequence.

Charles What does life hold for us, Edith? Tell me that. For me? A child I cannot acknowledge. A wife I no longer care for. And all because you wrote those letters. What's to be done?

Edith Do you regret the baby, Charles?

Charles (*confused*) Yes. No. I don't know. Mine, and yet not mine.

Edith You can see it whenever you like.

Charles It's not enough, Edith, *it's not enough*! I'm lost. A lawyer's brain is no use in a situation like this.

Edith Why don't you ask your sister's advice?

Charles You mean she ought to be told?

Edith I've no doubt Anna's told her already. Or Henry. The fact, I mean. The deduction she will have made for herself.

Charles And what am I to do about poor Anna? Must I stick by her?

Edith Your marriage need be no worse than many another. Mine isn't.

Charles (*bitterly*) What a comfort that is!

Edith I'm willing to go on with her education.

Charles You won't have the time. You'll have your own family now.

Charlotte enters. Sensing that something is in the wind, she looks quizzically from one to the other

Edith Hello, Charlotte.

Charlotte I thought I'd find you two here.

Edith So you deserted your new acquisition.

Charlotte Are you referring to Arnold?

Edith Of course.

Charlotte He's a pet. Much may be made of that man. I've decided to marry him.

Charles I thought you had.

Charlotte Well, Charles, you've got one foot in the Harnham business, so why shouldn't I?

Edith What do you mean by that, Charlotte?

Charlotte Your husband has just announced that the two of you are to have a baby.

Edith The two of us? I thought even he would have conceded that having a baby is woman's work.

Charlotte (*sternly*) Don't evade the issue, Edith. Was it the two of you?

Edith It's for you to speak, Charles.

Charles Edith says you will have made the deduction for yourself.

Charlotte Yes, I'm rather good at deductions.

Charles Then what should I do? You know I have always relied on your advice.

Charlotte Do? As little as possible. Outwardly, at least. It's a ridiculous situation you two have landed yourselves in. But you hardly need me to tell you that.

Edith Life is a ridiculous situation. Charles was my lover in spirit long before he married Anna.

Charlotte Society is interested in the flesh, not in the spirit.

Edith That part only goes back to the *County Arms*.

Charlotte The *County Arms* belongs to the past. What about the future?

Edith I'm not a prophetess.

Charles Links in a chain. From past to future. Links are forged by fate.

Charlotte You leave the links of fate to me. You need me around to keep an eye on you.

Edith Is that why you mean to marry Arnold?

Charlotte If you must have links of fate, he's one of them. I like Arnold. Besides, I'm getting on in years. It's about time I had someone to kick out of bed.

Edith And has he agreed to this arrangement?

Charlotte Don't worry about Arnold. I'm the one who makes the decisions.

Edith I don't doubt that.

Charles I'll have to go and rejoin Anna. For form's sake, you know. (*He takes Edith's hand*) We'll find a way, won't we?

Edith With Charlotte as an ally, I'm sure of it.

Charlotte Come along, Charles. Your wife will be waiting. (*She steers him towards the door*)

Charles and Charlotte exit

Edith shakes her head in wonderment and admiration as she watches them depart. After a moment or two, she sits at the desk, unlocks one of the drawers and produces a notebook and pen. She begins to write

Hardy enters, unnoticed by Edith

Hardy (*coughing*) I beg your pardon. Am I interrupting you?

Edith (*looking up; smiling*) Thomas. No, do come in.

Hardy (*closing the door quietly*) At last you call me Thomas. That makes me glad. Why have you not joined the others?

Edith (*closing the book*) I'll be in directly.

Hardy (*over her shoulder, reading the title*) "*The Year after the Fair*". What's that?

Edith My diary of the year's events. (*She locks it in the drawer from which she took it*) It's private and personal.

Hardy Don't worry, I'll not pry.

Edith (*smiling*) And you, Thomas, are perhaps the last person who ought to see it.

Hardy Why me of all people?

Edith You are a writer.

Hardy By which you mean I am a busybody?

Edith Writers take their material where they find it. You are like beach-combers scavenging the seashore.

Hardy It's surprising what the tide can leave behind. (*A pause*) May I congratulate you on the forthcoming event?

Edith Thank you.

Hardy Your husband is getting a little garrulous with drink. I've never seen him so before.

Edith He's a man who believes in moderation. (*A pause*) In all things.

Hardy Great news deserves a little excess.

Edith I'm glad he's pleased.

Hardy Shouldn't he be? Is it not the greatest event of his life?

Edith Evidently he thinks it is.

Hardy Precisely.

Edith And if he thinks it is, therefore it is.

Hardy Yours is a most interesting story, Edith.

Edith And would you tell it?

Hardy I know how to keep a confidence.

Edith How much do you know, Thomas?

Hardy Enough, I think. I'll be candid with you. I have been able to perform some small services for your husband. Yet I came into your lives by stealth.

Edith In quest of the missing piece in your jigsaw puzzle. And now it is complete.

Hardy The story of Charles and Anna Raye fascinated me. I wanted to know more.

Edith And found out a great deal more than you had bargained for, I think.

Hardy When I had become a regular visitor, your own marriage began to interest me as well. I hope you forgive my presumption.

Edith At least I understand it. You are a writer. It was fairly obvious my marriage was not one of my outstanding successes.

Hardy That applies to the married state itself.

Edith You are a pessimist.

Hardy I am an observer. I see the smiles. But I see beneath them as well.

Edith And are you going to tell the story?

Hardy I have told part of it already. I shall tell no more.

Edith Go on.

Hardy I have a book of short stories ready for the publishers. It's called *Life's Little Ironies*. I owe the phrase to yourself, Edith. It contains a trifle called *On the Western Circuit*. A story of a well-bred married lady who composed letters for an illiterate servant girl.

Edith And how does it end, this trifle?

Hardy With the servant's marriage.

Edith To the man on the Western Circuit?

Hardy Yes.

Edith And you say you will tell no more?

Hardy Not a word more on that particular subject.

Edith Now if I were a writer—and I only say if—I think I would say that the story cries out for a sequel.

Hardy You have all the instincts of a writer. But my own part is done. As I said, I know how to keep a confidence.

Edith I hope you will send me a copy of your book when it is published.

Hardy With great pleasure.

Edith You need not worry about my husband reading it. (*With a smile*) He's not interested in ... fiction.

Hardy I think we understand each other, Edith.

Edith I think we do, Thomas. Shall we rejoin the others now?

Hardy What about your diary?

Edith It can wait. It's safe in that drawer. I now have another interesting conversation to record.

Hardy After you, Edith.

She goes out, head held high. It is now Hardy's turn to shake his head in wonderment and admiration as he follows her

CURTAIN

FURNITURE AND PROPERTY LIST

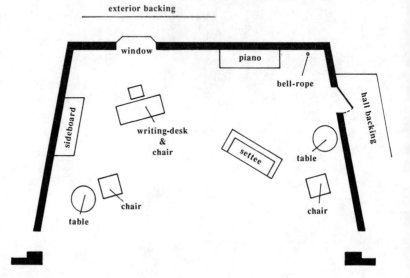

ACT I

Scene 1

On stage: Sideboard. *On it*: *objets d'art*
Low-backed settee. *On it*: newspaper for **Henry**
Writing desk. *On it*: writing materials, stamps, blotting paper. *In drawer*:
    notebook and pen
Desk chair
2 small tables
2 chairs
Heavy window curtains
Bell-rope
Piano (optional)
On walls: portraits and landscapes

Off stage: Nil

Personal: **Henry:** pocket-watch (required throughout)
    Anna: gloves, wedding-ring

SCENE 2

Strike: Newspaper, torn letter on writing desk

Off stage: Sheaf of papers **(Edith)**
              Card **(Betty)**
              Tray with two glasses and wine decanter **(Betty)**
              Sheaf of papers **(Edith)**

Personal: **Henry:** card

SCENE 3

Strike: Tray with glasses and wine decanter

Off stage: Tray with tea-things **(Betty)**

Personal: **Charlotte:** coin

SCENE 4

Strike: Tray with tea-things

Off stage: Nil

ACT II

SCENE 1

Set: Drinks for **Henry** and **Arnold**

Off stage: Newspaper **(Betty)**
              Book **(Betty)**

SCENE 2

Strike: Glasses

Set: Open window

Off stage: Nil

SCENE 3

On stage: As end of previous scene

Off stage: Nil

LIGHTING PLOT

Practical fittings required: *nil*

Interior. A drawing-room. The same scene throughout

ACT I, SCENE 1

To open: Effect of early afternoon light

No cues

ACT I, SCENE 2

To open: Effect of bright May morning

No cues

ACT I, SCENE 3

To open: Effect of early evening light

No cues

ACT I, SCENE 4

To open: Effect of mid-afternoon light

No cues

ACT II, SCENE 1

To open: Effect of afternoon light

No cues

ACT II, SCENE 2

To open: Effect of early evening light

No cues

ACT II, SCENE 3

To open: General interior lighting

No cues

EFFECTS PLOT

ACT I

Cue 1   **Henry:** "Well, we shall see."   (Page 3)
Sound of fly stopping, off

ACT II

Cue 2   **Henry:** "What I think is academic."   (Page 35)
Doorbell off

Cue 3   To open Scene 2   (Page 44)
Fairground music and voices, off

Cue 4   **Betty** closes the window   (Page 44)
Cut music

Cue 5   **Charlotte** opens the window   (Page 51)
Fairground music, off

Cue 6   **Charlotte** closes the window   (Page 52)
Cut music

MADE AND PRINTED IN GREAT BRITAIN BY
LATIMER TREND & COMPANY LTD PLYMOUTH

MADE IN ENGLAND